Key Stage 3 English Literacy Strategy Workbooks

These 3 books have been <u>written specifically</u> to follow the Literacy Strategy for KS3.

Each page has questions covering a Teaching Objective from the Literacy Strategy. Tips have also been included for some of the more difficult questions.

And there's even the odd ever-so-nearly entertaining bit, just to help keep you awake.

What CGP is all about

Our sole aim here at CGP is to produce the highest quality books — carefully written, immaculately presented and dangerously close to being funny.

Then we work our socks off to get them out to you — at the cheapest possible prices.

Contents

Section One — Spelling
Sorting Out Spelling 1
Review of Spelling Work 2
Review of Spelling Work — Rules 3
Tricky Beginnings and Endings 4
Revising Spelling Strategies 5
More Spelling Strategies 6
Checking Your Spelling 7

Section Two — Vocabulary
Words Used for Describing Language 8
Different Types of Meaning 9
Connectives 10

Section Three — Sentences and Paragraphs
Long Sentences 11
Punctuation 12
Writing — Getting the Style Right 13
Reporting What Someone Said 14
Paragraphs — Deciding What Goes Where 15

Section Four — Different Types of Non-Fiction
Formal or Informal 17
Non-Fiction — Writing Styles 18
ICT Texts 19

Section Five — Varieties of English
Standard English 20
Levels of Formality 21
Other Varieties of English 22
Language Change 23

Section Six — Research and Study Skills
Finding and Using Information 24
Collecting and Combining Information 25
Making and Using Notes 27
Can You Trust What You Read? 28
Evaluating Your Own Critical Writing 29
What About the Author? 30
Physical Differences in Presentation 31
The Influence of Readers 32

Section Seven — Author's Craft
Understanding the Author's Craft 33
Different Interpretations 34

Contents

   Author's Standpoint 35
   Rhetoric 36

Section Eight — Literary Texts
   Personal Response 37
   Analysing Drama Texts 38
   Historical Context 39
   American English 40
   Two Ways of Approaching a Theme 41
   Analysing Powerful Writing 42

Section Nine — Essay Skills
   Different Styles 43
   Writing an Article 44
   Formal Essays 45
   Formal Letters 46

Section Ten — Writing Fiction
   Writing Stories 47
   Adding Description 49
   Other Types of Entertaining Writing 50
   Different Types of Poetry 51

Section Eleven — Writing Information
   Writing Coherent Accounts 52
   Connecting Ideas 54
   Using Descriptive Detail 55
   Text Layout 56

Section Twelve — Writing to Persuade
   Using Adjectives 57
   Structuring an Argument 58
   Linking Arguments 59
   Giving Advice 60

Section Thirteen — Critical Writing
   Balanced Arguments 61
   Supporting Arguments 62
   Winning Arguments 63

Section Fourteen — Writing About Drama
   The Art of Performing 64
   Reading a Play 65
   Reviewing a Drama 66

   The Answers 67

Published by Coordination Group Publications Ltd.

Contributors:
Linda Bloor
Adrian Burke
Taissa Csáky
Mary Drayton
Gemma Hallam
Shona McIntosh
Alison Palin
Glenn Rogers
Jan Rumsey
Julie Schofield
James Paul Wallis
Jenny Watson
Chrissy Williams

Also Starring:
no goats, but a bit of a pheasant

With Thanks to:
Angela Ryder for the proofreading.

ISBN: 978 1 84146 134 2

Groovy website: www.cgpbooks.co.uk
Printed by Elanders Hindson Ltd, Newcastle upon Tyne.

Text, design, layout and original illustrations © Coordination Group Publications Ltd. 2002
All rights reserved.

Section One — Spelling

Sorting Out Spelling

There's lots about spelling rules in this section, but really one of the trickiest things is trying to remember how to spell random words that come up fairly often.

Q1 Each of the following sentences gives you a choice between two words. For each part below, say which word is spelt correctly.

   a)   There are lots of [deserts / desserts] in Africa.
   b)   Italy is a European [county / country].
   c)   I saw a shark once, in the Exe [estury / estuary].
   d)   London has a bit of trouble with [pollution / polution].
   e)   It depends [weather / whether] we get good [weather / whether].

Q2 Copy out the passage below, rewriting any words which are spelt incorrectly.

> Bob Angelo has been painting and drawing skeches for years. He is most famous for his colage showing Burger King in the forground of Venice. In particular, his use of acryllic paints highlites his incredible skill with a palate. His work is currently on exibition at the Tate Modern.

Hint: there are seven misspelt words.

Maths has some pretty nasty spellings to remember — most coming from either Greek or Latin.

Q3 In the following sentences you are given a choice between two spellings for each mathematical word. Say which is the correct spelling.

   a)   A triangle can be [equilateral / equilaterel], [isoseles / isosceles] or [scalene / skalene].
   b)   The shape has [reflecional / reflectional] [symmetry / symmetrey].
   c)   The [paralelogram / parallelogram] and [rombus / rhombus] are examples of [quadralaterals / quadrilaterals].
   d)   Distance is [mesured / measured] in [metres / meters], and mass in [tonnes / tonns].
   e)   The [horizontal / horazontal] is [perpandicular / perpendicular] to the [virtical / vertical].

These next words are pretty tricky, but at least they're all spelt right.

Q4 The underlined word in each of the following sentences has somehow ended up in the **wrong** sentence. Rewrite each sentence correctly so it makes sense.

   a)   The brothers always <u>siege</u> each other.
   b)   The Houses of <u>immigration</u> are in London.
   c)   King Mordred laid <u>civilisation</u> to Paris.
   d)   It can be difficult to move to Australia because of the <u>chronological</u> laws.
   e)   An alien <u>contradict</u> could be very advanced.
   f)   The story is told in <u>Parliament</u> order.

Section One — Spelling

Review of Spelling Work

On the next three pages is some stuff about spelling that you've probably covered before — but when did a bit of revision ever hurt...?

It's quite often the vowels (-a, -e, -i, -o, -u) that are the tricky parts.

Q1 Look at the words below. What do you notice about the sound the underlined vowels make?

  abr**o**ad
  s**ou**rce
  s**au**ce

No wonder it's difficult getting the right spelling for these parts of a word. You need to know the different sounds that vowels make, on their own and grouped together. Also, use the strategies on pages 5 and 6 to help you learn and check problem words.

Q2 For each of the words below, write down at least five other words which have the same vowel sound in them. Try to use as many different combinations of letters as you can to make the same sound. I've done the first one for you.

  a) deep
  a) *cream, cede, ceiling, demon, key*
  b) dry
  c) bird
  d) here
  e) chair

Q3 Complete each of the words below by putting the correct vowels in the spaces. For some of them, you should be able to find two or three possible vowels or pairs of vowels to complete different words.

  a) s - y
  b) s t - - d
  c) a l t h - - g h
  d) b - t t e r
  e) l - v e l y
  f) l - n e l y
  g) l - g h t
  h) h - - g h t*
  i) w - - g h t*

  j) w - - t
  k) r e l - - f*
  l) r e c - - v e*
  m) w - - r d*
  n) b - - - t i f u l
  o) w - m - n
  p) g - v e n
  q) j - l l y
  r) j - - l o u s

Most words follow the *i* before *e* except after *c* rule, but there are exceptions.

Q4 Which of the words in Q3 marked with a * **don't** follow the rule?

I likes spelling I do — but not me grammar...

There's a deep-green demon on the ceiling and he's seething because we keep fiendishly stealing his meek, sleek sneakers. Hmm. It's no wonder so many people have trouble with spelling is it really...

Section One — Spelling

Review of Spelling Work — Rules

Spelling rules can be a real help with some groups of words. Although there are often exceptions to these rules, they are still useful for most words.

Rule: if the word has one syllable, ends in a consonant and the consonant has **one** vowel before it, double the last letter when adding **-ed** or **-ing**.

Q1 Add **-ed** and **-ing** onto each of the words below, remembering to follow the rule:

- a) tag
- b) drop
- c) shop
- d) hum
- e) prod
- f) step
- g) net
- h) jog

Exceptions to this rule are words ending in **-w** and **-y** — you don't double these letters.

Rule: when words end in the suffix **-ful** (e.g. careful, helpful), double the **l** when you add **-y** e.g. carefu*ll*y, helpfu*ll*y.

Rule: if a word ends in **-y** and has a consonant before the **y**, change the **y** to an **i** when you add a suffix. The suffix **-ing** is an exception to this rule — you keep the **y**.

Q2 Look at the following examples and then complete the words below them in the same way:

adjectives: **happy**   **happier**   **happiest**
- a) lazy   laz - - -   laz - - - -
- b) flashy   flash - - -   flash - - - -

verb endings: **justify**   **justifies**   **justified**
- c) multiply   multipl - - -   multipl - - -
- d) qualify   qualif - - -   qualif - - -

Rule: to change a noun from **singular** (one) to **plural** (more than one), we usually just add **-s**.
e.g. house — hou*s*e*s*, tree — tree*s*
Exceptions to this rule:
  if the word ends in **-s, -ch, -ss, -sh** or **-x**, add **-es**.
  if a word ends in **-y**, change the **-y** to an **-i**, and then add **-es**.
  some nouns change the letters in the word to make it plural.
e.g. mouse — mice
   man — men
   woman — women

*But remember — if there's a vowel right before the **-y**, just add **-s**.*

Q3 Using the rules above, write out the plural of each of these words:

- a) story
- b) fox
- c) kite
- d) quantity
- e) bus
- f) march
- g) kiss
- h) frequency
- i) spy
- j) wish
- k) laboratory
- l) louse

Section One — Spelling

Tricky Beginnings and Endings

It's easy to mix up prefixes that **mean** the same thing, like **dis-**, **mis-**, **il-**, **im-**, **in-**, **ir-** and **un-**. You can also get in a muddle with endings that **sound** very similar, like **-able** and **-ible**.

Q1 Choose the correct prefix from the box on the right to give each of these words its opposite meaning. I've done the first one for you.

a) please
displease
b) necessary
c) moral
d) understood
e) satisfied
f) legal
g) discreet
h) regular

dis-
il-
im-
in-
ir-
mis-
un-

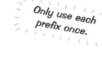
Only use each prefix once.

Q2 Say which word out of each of the following pairs is spelt correctly:

a) He was a [formidible / formidable] opponent.
b) Terry wants a [collapsible / collapsable] bicycle.
c) The giant killer robot mouse was virtually [invincible / invincable].
d) The water here is [undrinkible / undrinkable].
e) It's pointless to fight the [inevitible / inevitable].

Q3 Add either **-ary** or **-ery** to complete the words below (I've put the meanings in brackets):

a) cemet... (*place where people are buried*)
b) station... (*standing still / not moving*)
c) station... (*paper, pens, pencils, etc.*)
d) diction... (*book containing the definitions of words*)
e) confection... (*sweets and chocolate, mmmm...*)

Q4 Add either **-ence** or **-ance** to complete each of these nouns:

a) differ.... (*that which isn't the same*)
b) confer.... (*a meeting where people discuss things*)
c) accept.... (*willingness to accept*)
d) brilli.... (*outstanding talent*)
e) relev.... (*extent that something applies to the matter in hand*)

Q5 Finish off these words using either **-cian**, **-sion**, **-ssion**, **-tian** or **-tion**:

a) Egyp... (*person / thing from Egypt*)
b) colli... (*crash / violent impact*)
c) discu... (*conversation*)
d) opti... (*eye-doctor*)
e) emo... (*e.g. love, hate, ambivalence [I like that word], etc.*)

"Does my bum look big in this?"

Section One — Spelling

Revising Spelling Strategies

A mnemonic is something that helps your memory. It could be a phrase where each word represents one letter of the word you're trying to remember.

e.g.	**goes**	grotty old egg sandwiches
	rhythm	rhythm has your two hips moving
	island	an island *is land*

Q1 Create your own mnemonics for:
- a) does
- b) rhyme
- c) jealous

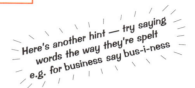

Here's another hint — try saying words the way they're spelt e.g. for business say bus-i-ness

Another useful type of mnemonic is a sentence which acts as a memory jogger, like this one for the word 'environment':
En, Vi, Ron — men that care about the **environment**.

Q2 Write down some similar sentences for **three** words which you have difficulty spelling.

You can break words up into chunks so that they are easier to remember.

Q3 Say how you would break up the following words. Why have you chosen to break them up in that way?
- a) miscellaneous
- b) furthermore
- c) necessitate
- d) embarrassing
- e) interesting
- f) parallel
- g) perpendicular

There are no 'right' or 'wrong' answers to this question. It's here to help you work out your own strategies for remembering these words.

You can also look out for common endings in particular word families, e.g. words ending in **-or** *like doct**or**, act**or** and profess**or**, are often professions.*

Q4 Put the words below into six groups. The words in each group should all end with the same letters and belong to the same family of words.

magician physicist happier telescope biology electrician easier capricious physician
outrageous dentist sociology kaleidoscope ferocious optician psychology angrier
cosmology microscope delicious periscope musician malicious friendlier physiotherap**ist**

Remember, remember, the 5th of — erm, oh...

The main thing is to try and work out your own ways of remembering all these spellings. They'll serve you through your whole life and zzzzzzzzzzzzzz...

Section One — Spelling

More Spelling Strategies

Look for a spelling link with another word,
*e.g. envir*o*nment and gover*n*ment*

For words that sound similar but are spelt differently (homophones), you can make up helpful sayings e.g. for their / there confusions: Their heir could be here or there.

Think carefully about patterns, tricky endings, silent letters and word origins.

*It can be helpful to think about **patterns** in words.*

Q1 For each group of words below, write down how the words are similar. What does this tell you about the meaning?

    a) necessary necessarily necessity necessitate
    b) vision visual visualise visionary
    c) argue argument arguable arguably
    d) differ different differently difference
    e) know knowingly knowledgeable unknown
    f) resist resistive resistance irresistible

*When you add a suffix to a word ending in a silent **e** you have to decide whether or not to drop the **e**. The basic rule is that you drop the **e** if the suffix begins with a vowel, and keep it if the suffix begins with a consonant — but there are exceptions.*

Q2 For each of the following circumstances, say whether you would keep the **e** or drop it.

    a) when a word ends in **-ce** or **-ge** (e.g. notice) and you're adding **-able** or **-ous**
    b) when you're adding a **-y**
    c) when the word ends **-ye**, **-oe**, or **-ee** (e.g. agree)

Q3 Write down five words that contain each of the following silent letters. I've given you a hint for each one in brackets:

    a) **k** (always before **n** — beginning of the word)
    b) **w** (before **r** or **h** — beginning of the word)
    c) **gh** (at the end of a word or before **t**)
    d) **e** (at the end of a word)
    e) **h** (at the beginning of a word or after **r**)
    f) **b** (after **m** or before **t**)
    g) **p** (always before **s**, **n**, or **t** — these words all come from Greek)

Some words are difficult because they come from other languages.

Q4 Write out the Latin plural for each of these words (some have English plurals too):

    a) axis
    b) medium
    c) formula
    d) hippopotamus

Latin endings can be a bit tricky to remember, but you need to know them for Science.

Section One — Spelling

Checking Your Spelling

You can always use a **dictionary** to check any spellings you're not sure about. Remember to use the headwords at the top of each page to help you find the right section quickly. If you can't find the word, try different letter patterns that make the same sound, e.g. **f** / **ph**. When you find what you're looking for, it's always a good idea to check the meaning of the word.

If you word-process your work, a **spellchecker** can be useful, but remember: spellcheckers won't sort out problems with homophones or word confusions. They'll give you choices that you need to check on carefully before you make your decision.

Q1   How many spelling errors can you find in the sentence below?

>   Their where lots of freinds inn you're house last knight.

Now type the sentence into a word-processor and run the spellchecker on it. How many mistakes did it identify?

Q2   The words below are spelt incorrectly. Write out the correct spellings for each:
   a)   biskit   h)   puppys
   b)   nife   i)   leafs
   c)   rubarb   j)   wellcome
   d)   recieve   k)   traveling
   e)   churchs   l)   loveing
   f)   sheild   m)   managable
   g)   potatos   n)   cryed

Q3   Say which word out of each pair below is spelt correctly:
   a)   It's clearly an [amphibian / amfibian].
   b)   It's certainly not a [mammel / mammal].
   c)   How can you tell if it's a [vertabrate / vertebrate]?
   d)   Get a load of those [triceps / triseps].
   e)   I don't like the [composition / composicion] of that picture.
   f)   His tongue is twelve [kilometres / kilometers] long.
   g)   My guess is that he's [foreign / foriegn].

Wot do you meen? — my spelchequer wokrs fine...

Yes, yes, yes, you've heard it all before I know, but spellcheckers are **NOT** the be-all and end-all. You've still got to check it all through yourself to make sure you haven't made any missedaches.

Section One — Spelling

Section Two — Vocabulary

Words Used for Describing Language

*Language is made up of many different types of words and groups of words.
When you're describing language, you need to be able to identify these different words.*

Q1 Match the following definitions with the correct words from the box. The first one has been done for you.

a) word that tells you what someone / something is doing or being

 verb

b) clause which can stand by itself and make sense
c) word which modifies another word, e.g. tells you more about the verb
d) word used for naming a person, place, animal or thing
e) describing word which tells you more about a noun or pronoun
f) verb which shows that the subject of the sentence is having the action done to it
g) clause which can't stand by itself and make sense

noun	adjective	verb	passive verb
main clause	subordinate clause	adverb	

Q2 Look back to the words in the box in Q1.
Write down an example of each from the passage below.

> Yesterday we all went for a trip on the canal boat. It was an absolutely gorgeous day and so we just took off, not even bothering to pack a picnic. We knew we'd pass some pubs and we had enough provisions on board to make snacks and drinks. A great time was had by all, and we were sorry when we got back to the boatyard. The children would have liked to spend the night on the boat, but unfortunately both David and I had to go to work today. We agreed we should do it again, though.

As well as being able to describe the types of words used in a text, you need to be able to spot different writing **techniques**.

Q3 Each of the following sentences contains an example of one of the items from the box. Match up the sentences with the correct item.

a) She's obviously not as clever as you.
b) Peter pointedly placed a piece of pepperoni on his plate.
c) He's as white as a sheet.
d) He squelched through the mud.
e) How can I compete with this giant?
f) I thought I saw the tall one yawn this morning.

alliteration
assonance
comparison
metaphor
simile
onomatopoeia

Grammar we love you — grammar we do...

Fun it ain't, but learn it you must. If you're struggling with this (most people do), get a fresh sheet of paper, write down all of the technical words on this page, then scribble down what they mean. Keep doing it until you get them all right. Then do these questions again and they'll be much easier.

Different Types of Meaning

There are often lots of different ways of making the same point.

Q1 Write down the following sentences and match them to the correct explanation from the box.

    a) Jane was not the easiest person in the world to live with.
    b) Elizabeth has firm principles.
    c) Jack always has a great deal to say for himself.
    d) Custard isn't her favourite food.
    e) He has limited experience in this field.
    f) The government is considering the differing views which have been expressed.
    g) It's well known that the two men do not have an easy relationship.

> can't stand each other
> really doesn't like it
> hasn't decided what to do
> difficult to get on with
> talks too much
> stubborn
> knows hardly anything about it

Q2 For each of the following sentences, write down a shorter sentence which says the same thing in a more direct way.

    a) Would you like to get your books out, please?
    b) I suggest you start at the beginning.
    c) I'd rather you didn't do that.

*Many words have **different meanings** in different contexts.*

Q3 For each of the underlined words below, write down its meaning in the sentence here. Also give an alternative meaning of the word.

    a) He was tired of all the <u>spin</u> and sleaze in politics.
    b) The <u>fallout</u> from these events is going to be considerable.
    c) The <u>road</u> to peace would not be easy.
    d) She works on the European <u>desk</u>.

Phrases *can have more than one meaning too.*

Q4 a) Rewrite the following pairs of sentences, using one phrase from the box to fill in the gaps in both sentences.

    i) They were ... nervously.
       It's no use MPs ... now.
    ii) We decided to ..., at the pub.
       We're going to have to ... on this.
    iii) They were ... the sofa.
        They've been ... these documents for months.
    iv) I'm just finishing ... .
        Her new job's ... .
    v) The first runner was ... when he slipped.
       He won't be ... just yet.
    vi) Wispy clouds were ... .
        She left her remark ..., and disappeared.

> meet them halfway
> sitting on
> the icing on the cake
> wringing their hands
> hanging in the air
> handing over the baton

    b) Write down a sentence which means the same as the second sentence in each of the pairs above.

Section Two — Vocabulary

Connectives

*The words and phrases in the box below are examples of **connectives**.*
These can be used to link sentences together.

Q1 Write down all the words from the box which you could use to do the following:

    a)   put an opposite / different view
    b)   say more of the same, or say something which backs up what you've just written
    c)   write about something which happened because of the thing you've just written about
    d)   write about something which happened at a later time

consequently	in spite of this	because of this...
furthermore	despite this	as a result of this...
subsequently	although	a consequence of this was...
moreover	following the...	later...
however	in addition to this...	nevertheless

The words you choose to link your ideas give the reader a clue
to what's coming next. This makes your writing easier to read.

Q2 The following sentences all have the wrong endings.
Rearrange the underlined parts so that the sentences make sense.

    a)   You look upstairs while <u>Jack had started the next one</u>.
    b)   In order to allow us to check our records, <u>we can tick you off on the register</u>.
    c)   In general it seems quite good, although <u>we'll start without him</u>.
    d)   I won't be able to help you unless <u>I check if he's outside</u>.
    e)   We need to know your name so that <u>I can't comment on the details</u>.
    f)   Since he hasn't arrived, <u>please fill in your details below</u>.
    g)   Jane was still finishing the first exercise. Meanwhile, <u>you tell me what the problem is</u>.

Q3 Complete the following sentences by adding appropriate endings.

    a)   Even though he liked football,
    b)   First sieve the flour, then
    c)   We won't be able to go unless
    d)   The job was well within his capabilities. Furthermore,
    e)   He began his career at Leicester City and subsequently
    f)   I am aware of the special circumstances surrounding this case. Nevertheless,

Connectives — why use words — dashes are much better...

To be able to link your sentences together, you need to know a few <u>connectives</u>. Try to remember all the ones in the box above — that way you'll never be stuck for a way of linking your sentences into one long, flowing, endless passage of beautiful writing... or you could use dashes like I do.

Section Two — Vocabulary

Section Three — Sentences and Paragraphs

Long Sentences

Varying the structure of your sentences is a good way of making your writing more interesting. To do this properly, you need to know how to join the different bits of sentences together.

Q1 **Join the two halves of each sentence together, and then write out the sentences:**

- a) I asked her to phone me
- b) Please let us know
- c) How would you like it
- d) These are the things you'll need
- e) I don't know why he came
- f) Having seen the photos

    - i) if it happened to you?
    - ii) , I wish I'd been there.
    - iii) — he knew we were okay.
    - iv) if we can be of any further assistance.
    - v) : pyjamas, underwear, sleeping bag, soap, toothpaste, toothbrush and comb.
    - vi) as soon as she arrived.

Tip — pay attention to the punctuation.

Sometimes it's clearer to break long sentences up into shorter ones.

Q2 **Rewrite each of these rambling sentences as a group of shorter sentences:**

- a) The unfortunate animal was eventually found in its hiding place, which was halfway up a tree at the bottom of the garden, and brought back down after a neighbour lent an extra long ladder which was only just long enough to reach the cat, which by now was absolutely terrified.

- b) I phoned the station yesterday to ask about train times; actually, I phoned twice because you often get told different things; then I rang Lucy who told me she'd been told something completely different — in fact, what she'd been told was different from the two pieces of information I'd received.

- c) There weren't enough parents to help with transport, so we couldn't go on the trip, which was a shame really as the whole class apart from Jack was looking forward to it even though we'd heard some pretty scary stories about white-water rafting; in fact, I'm not sure why Jack was scared as he's usually one of the most adventurous in the class and will generally have a go at anything.

*When reviewing long sentences, ask yourself:
Does it make sense?
Is it properly punctuated?
Is it ambiguous?*

Q3 **Write down the sentences which are TRUE:**

- a) Long sentences are fine as long as your meaning is clear.
- b) When putting clauses together, you should check what punctuation, if any, is needed.
- c) Often a short sentence is clearer and more effective than a long one.
- d) The longer the sentence, the more impressed the examiner will be.
- e) If you get bored or lost halfway through writing a sentence, so will your reader.

Learning about sentences is fun — true or false...

My cat's <u>never</u> got stuck up a tree. She did fall in the canal once though. She just arrived at the door, wailing and looking all bedraggled. Poor thing — she was in a mood for the whole evening.

Section Three — Sentences and Paragraphs

Punctuation

If you punctuate your writing properly, it'll be easy to understand and much more effective.

Q1 Write down this list of punctuation marks and their symbols. From the list on the right, choose suitable reasons / places for using each punctuation mark, and write these next to the relevant punctuation mark.

comma ,
full stop .
question mark ?
exclamation mark !
semicolon ;
colon :

i) between sentences
ii) between some clauses
iii) after a question
iv) after a sentence which is very emphatic
v) between items in a list
vi) to introduce something, for example a list
vii) between sentences which you want to join together
viii) before direct speech

*Commas have lots of uses, but joining sentences together isn't one of them (unless the comma is followed by a word like **so**, **but**, or **because**).*

Q2 Rewrite these sentences, changing the comma to a semicolon or dash:

a) Don't worry if you can't come, we'll send you what you need.
b) I'll get your coat, don't forget to pick up your bags.
c) Metals are good conductors, non-metals are good insulators.
d) There will be several room changes this week, please consult the lists on the noticeboards.
e) Don't download your e-mail, your virus protection isn't up to date.

Remember that dashes are more informal than semicolons.

Q3 Some of these sentences need commas to make them clearer. Some have commas where there shouldn't be one. Write out the sentences, removing or adding commas as necessary.

a) My mother who's seventy-six can remember the war.
b) I'd like to see Jane Phil and Peter after assembly.
c) Could anyone who has seen my camera, please tell me?
d) If you ask I'm sure he'll help you.
e) Could you remind me, to water the plants before we go?
f) However we do this it won't be easy.
g) He's convinced it's the right thing to do. However I'm not.

Q4 Write out these sentences about colons, followed by the correct example from the list below:

a) You can use a colon before a list.
b) You can use a colon before a quotation, especially a long one.
c) A colon is sometimes used to show that an explanation, or more information, is about to be given.

i) He told me there was no need to worry: he had examined her and decided that a trip to hospital was not necessary.
ii) You'll need the following: a packed lunch, drinks, spare clothes and a sunhat.
iii) To paraphrase a friend of mine: some people live a long time before realising that they're actually very happy.

Section Three — Sentences and Paragraphs

Writing — Getting the Style Right

The style of your writing should vary with the context.

Q1 Copy out the table below. Put each word (a to j) in the correct column. After you've done this, complete the table by filling in the remaining blanks. I've done the first one for you.

a) isn't
b) wasn't
c) notwithstanding
d) moreover
e) facilitate
f) reprimand
g) ensure
h) in-your-face
i) nevertheless
j) wicked (=brilliant)

	More formal	Less formal
a)	is not	isn't
b)		
c)		
d)		
e)		
f)		
g)		
h)		
i)		
j)		

Passive verbs can be a useful way of getting your message across in more formal writing.

Q2 Pair up these sentences, so that the same thing is being said in two different ways:

a) The matter was discussed at length.
b) The full effects of using this medicine have not yet been properly investigated.
c) A new peace deal has been brokered.
d) More goods are imported than are exported.
e) Germany was reunified in 1990.
f) A decision was finally reached, but not before several points of view had been aired.

i) No one's tried to find out the effects of this medicine yet.
ii) They've sorted out a new peace deal.
iii) We had a really long talk about the whole thing.
iv) They import more than they export.
v) They joined Germany together again in 1990.
vi) We finally reached a decision, but only after hearing lots of opinions.

Another way of successfully presenting ideas in formal writing is through the use of nouns instead of verbs.

Q3 Copy out the more formal sentence from each pair:

a) Further work remains to be done.
   We still need to work on this.

b) A lot of industries started around this time.
   The growth of new industries continued throughout this period.

c) Of course people will be consulted.
   Consultation with the public will, of course, continue.

Evil Dictator Phil's plans to wipe out the human race would remain as democratic as possible.

Section Three — Sentences and Paragraphs

Reporting What Someone Said

You use speech marks when you're writing down someone's exact words, but not if you're just talking about what they said.

Q1 Have a look at the example below, then write out each sentence (a to f) with the correct punctuation:

Mr Brown said he regretted the situation.
"Obviously I regret what has happened," said Mr Brown.

a) I really adored chocolate when I was young, said Deirdre.
b) Deirdre declared her childhood love of chocolate.
c) Neither of us did it, said the boys.
d) Both parties maintained their innocence.
e) You know I'll love you forever, she murmured.
f) She told him she would always love him.

Q2 Write down the sentences below in two lists, under the headings: **exact words** and **not necessarily exact words**.

a) He said she was lazy and uncooperative.
b) He called him a "shining example".
c) They threatened to call a referendum.
d) She says he's working too hard.
e) Members have called for "a fresh approach".

Q3 Copy out the passage below, filling in the gaps with phrases from the box. Remember to use speech marks where necessary.

| Can I see them? | the father was a labrador | Of course, |
| Puppies for Sale | there were four puppies | |

As I walked along the High Street, I noticed a sign in the village shop saying .... I pushed open the door and went in. The woman behind the counter told me .... who were three weeks old. She said .... and the mother was a retriever. .... I asked. .... she replied, and led me through a door at the back of the shop.

Q4 These sentences all contain the exact words that someone said. Write out the sentences, punctuating them correctly.

a) In the final chapter, the hero is described as a man without hope.
b) He referred to him as a callous and insensitive coward.
c) She said later that he should mind his own business.
d) They used to call me Forgetful Flo because of my terrible memory.

Speech marks — I'd give Mr Blair 7 out of 10...

Two things to learn: 1) when to use speech marks and when to leave well alone, and 2) how to use speech marks when you need them. Loads of people get this stuff wrong — make sure you don't.

Section Three — Sentences and Paragraphs

Paragraphs — Deciding What Goes Where

You need to start a new paragraph when you start writing about something different.

Q1 Look at this text:

> Cats make ideal pets. They're affectionate, but won't miss you if you pop out for a few hours without them. They're clean, and won't make a mess in your house — as long as they can get through the cat flap, or know how to use the litter tray. They're delicate and graceful, and will make a gentle purring noise to show their contentment. Dogs, on the other hand, are a completely different story. Yes, they're affectionate — so affectionate that they'll bark hysterically if you dare to leave the house without them. Then they'll bark hysterically if you dare to come home. And on rainy days they'll bring mud — and goodness knows what else — into your house.

a) Write down the sentence which should start the second paragraph.

b) Write down the **single word** which shows you that the writer has switched to talking about something different.

c) Write down **two phrases** which show you that the writer has switched to talking about something different.

The writer of the passage below has successfully separated his ideas into paragraphs.

Q2 Fill in the table so that it shows how each paragraph begins, and what each paragraph is talking about. Use the phrases from the box.

Paragraph	Begins	Talks about
1		
2		
3		
4		

To be even more radical…
If you have satellite…
Most families argue…
An alternative to arguing…

alternative solution — don't watch TV
more radical solution — don't have TV
further problem — satellite TV
basic problem — arguing over TV — + solutions

Most families argue about what to watch on the telly. The solution to this problem is a) to persuade your mum to buy everyone their own TV set, b) to watch something that no one really wants to see, just to be fair, or c) to encourage your brothers and sisters to go round to their friends' houses as often as possible (or, better still, to go and live there).

If you have satellite, the problem is even worse. How does anyone have time to read the telly guide for all those channels, never mind actually watch all the programmes?

An alternative to arguing about programmes is to turn off the TV. Instead, you could play a game such as chess or Scrabble. At the same time, you could talk about your day at school. Then you could go and finish your homework, start your maths assignment, or read a book.

To be even more radical, you could choose not to have a TV. However, the problem with the no-telly approach is that you'll get regular visits from the TV detector people. They won't believe that you don't have a telly in the house and will want to know why you don't have a licence.

Paragraphs — Deciding What Goes Where

The first sentence of each paragraph helps the reader to know what the paragraph will be about.

Q1 In this paragraph, the sentences are mixed up:

Don't forget that a hard floor is much noisier and colder than a carpet. Of course, you can have the best of both worlds by using rugs on top of a hard surface. Do you need something that is easily cleaned (a hard floor), or something that is warm and comfortable (a soft carpet)? When choosing a new floor covering, consider the following points:

a) Write out the sentence which should come first.

b) Write out the rest of the paragraph in a sensible order.

c) Write down three words which gave you a clue to your answer for a).

The first sentence should also provide a link with the previous paragraph.

Q2 Read the passage below. Write down what the first sentence of each paragraph refers back to.

    Later that day Peter phoned me again. He wanted to know why Janet was behaving so strangely. Apparently she'd refused to go out, even though it was his birthday. She said she had a headache. He was a bit surprised that she wanted him to stay in with her.

    As soon as Peter was off the phone, I rang Janet. I told her she needed to be a bit more convincing and that Peter was getting suspicious. She asked for some advice on how to tell better lies — like I would know! I gave her some tips, though.

    My advice must have worked — Janet managed to keep it a secret. Peter said later that he really had no idea. At one point he phoned to say he'd be late home, and we started to worry that he wouldn't come to his own party.

    He finally arrived — and the party was a big success. Loads of people were there, and a great time was had by all. Phew.

The first sentence of a paragraph should usually link to the paragraph before.

Q3 Which of these are good reasons for including a sentence in a paragraph? Write them down.

a) It leads on from the first sentence.
b) It develops or gives more detail about the point in the first sentence.
c) It illustrates or supports the point in the first sentence.
d) It talks about something that happened around the same time.
e) You just thought of it and want to write it down before you forget about it.

Don't worry if some paragraphs are short — don't waffle on for the sake of it.

Q4 These paragraphs only contain two sentences each. Match the halves, and write them out:

a) There are several ways to get in touch with us.
b) As he walked along the street he had a sudden sense of having been there before.
c) Later that day he received a text message from his girlfriend.

i) But he did not recognise the stone buildings or cobbled road surfaces.
ii) She wanted some help with her homework.
iii) You can phone us, send us a text or e-mail, fax us, or even put a letter in the post.

Section Three — Sentences and Paragraphs

Section Four — Different Types of Non-Fiction

Formal or Informal

Read Ali's informal description of the Shetland Islands:

The Shetland Islands are a group of islands just up from, and a bit right of, the Orkneys. In the 9th century, those Norse types sneaked in and took over the islands. Then in 1472, Scotland nicked them. The people do loads of fishing, and the islands are famous for those cute little Shetland Ponies.

Q1 a) Copy out the description, underlining the informal parts.

b) Rewrite Ali's description so that it could be an entry in an encyclopedia.

Q2 Say whether you should use formal or informal language for writing each of the following:

a) a letter applying for a part-time job
b) your own web page containing all the gossip and funny stories from school
c) a report about a school concert for the local newspaper

*Read the following passage. In it, the writer uses **formal** language to describe his day out at a castle.*

> Last Saturday I had a very pleasant day out at Craggyskello Castle. The castle is situated approximately ten miles from the nearest dwelling in the depths of Cumbria. According to the locals, Craggyskello was constructed in 1227 by an incredibly insane landowner who felt his house was not strong enough to protect him from an attack by the vicious mountain sheep. After his death, the castle was used as a base for resisting invasion from the Millomians. A most pleasing feature of the castle was a remarkable curved turret. However, more impressive were the dungeons, accessed via a long, winding staircase which goes deep underground. The walls were covered in slime and we saw several skeletons of prisoners who had died there. The only light came from our torches and I have to say that I felt quite uncomfortable. Back above ground, there were also some extremely beautiful gardens, in which the present owner grows a multitude of flowers and vegetables. All in all it was a great day out and I highly recommend it.

Q3 Imagine you've just been on a trip to Craggyskello Castle and really enjoyed it. The castle owners are trying to attract more young people and have asked you to write an account of your day at the castle. Rewrite the above description in a way that will encourage other kids to visit. I've started it for you.

e.g. Last Saturday I went to Craggyskello Castle. It was the best day out — ever!

Well — that was page 17...

Goes without saying, but you should probably not start your job application letter "Hi Jon, just wondered if you've got any jobs going — bit skint at the moment so I figured I'd best get a job..."

Non-Fiction — Writing Styles

Read this note from a factory foreman to the operations manager:

> Bob,
> Thought I'd better let you know there was a bit of an incident last night, (2.20am). 'Lucky' Williams (that's his nickname — his real name is Len) lost part of his finger working on assembly line B. Couldn't find it. Checked all around the conveyer belt. No one from health and safety available. We were canning the extra hot chilli sauce last night. He's in Evergreen Hospital now, and they say he'll be okay — it's not too bad. He's in ward 3F. The others on the assembly line were a bit upset, so I let them go early, provided they didn't tell anyone why.
> Have a good day.
> Ron.

Q1 Imagine you are Bob Honeysilk, the operations manager. Write a report for the health and safety officer, using the relevant information from the foreman's note. You'll have to think of a full name for the foreman, and for the health and safety officer. Add any other information you think necessary (use the following ideas to help you).

- the factory's previous safety record
- Len Williams' previous safety record
- verbal reports from witnesses
- doctor's reports from the hospital
- recommendations regarding informing the staff or the public
- recommendations about sick pay and compensation

The local newspaper has found out about the missing finger. It has started a campaign to find the can containing the finger. The person who finds it will get a reward and the chance to meet 'Lucky' Len Williams.

Q2 Write the first newspaper article for the campaign. Remember to include an eye-catching headline. You could also include a quote from Len or Bob.

Since the incident, the company have gone safety-mad. They've even decided to put a list of 'safe can-opening' instructions on the side of each can.

Q3 Write this list of instructions as simply as you can.

'Lucky' Len Williams has decided to set up his own insurance claims company. (As you do.)

Q4 Think of a company name for him, and write a 30-second radio advertisement promoting his new company.

Ewww — kind of gone off chilli sauce now...

Don't rush this page — think about each style of writing (look at some examples) before you start your answers. You use different styles for a newspaper (sensationalist, dramatic, exaggerating), a set of instructions (clear, direct, numbered points), adverts (designed to sell something), and so on.

Section Four — Different Types of Non-Fiction

ICT Texts

ICT stands for **Information Communication Technology**. ICT texts are things like web pages, e-mails, etc.

Q1 Write down as many forms of communication technology as you can which exist today, but which didn't exist 50 years ago.

Q2 A full-colour world atlas can be presented in different forms. Write down an advantage and disadvantage of each of the following forms:

    a)   a book
    b)   a CD-ROM

Imagine your school is completely new, and is going to have a school website. Students, teachers, parents and prospective parents will be the main users of the site.

Q3 Write a short description of how you would design the website. Make sure you think about each of the following:

— what information each of the groups of readers will need
— how you would organise the information
— using pictures and / or sound
— including links to other sites (if so, which sites?)

Q4 'All e-mail messages should be correctly spelt and punctuated.' Do you agree? Think about the different ways e-mails are used and then write your answer.

*Most e-mails to friends are written in an **informal** way. Read the following e-mail:*

> hiya Tony
>
> just wondering if you're up for coming round to mine to watch the footie tonight. should be a cracking match — can't wait to see liverpool hammer utd, again (one day you'll see the error of your ways!!). anyway, i've got loads of friends coming round so you won't stay miserable for long!
>
> see you later mate
> Phil

Q5 Now imagine that Phil also decides to invite his Man Utd supporting uncle, Dave, who he only sees occasionally. Rewrite the above e-mail so that Phil could send it to Dave. Remember to use more formal language and the correct punctuation.

Section Four — Different Types of Non-Fiction

Section Five — Varieties of English

Standard English

Q1 It's important to use standard English in your written work. Rewrite the following sentences using standard English.

   a) I done better than I expected.

   b) They was waiting for someone to help them.

   c) I were right.

   d) She were still hungry.

   e) It don't have to be like this.

   f) I seen him yesterday.

   g) Jane done it.

   h) I ain't never seen it.

   i) Her give it me.

   j) I'll do it after.

   k) The man what came yesterday were a bit strange.

   In informal conversations people often use words and expressions which aren't suitable in formal contexts.

Q2 Rewrite these sentences, so that they are less informal:

   a) He said it was a pile of pants.

   b) She finished them dead quick.

   c) He said he'd come round ours fiveish.

   d) John's new wheels are right smart.

   e) Nah, I was checking out the other one, innit.

   f) Chuck us a packet of crisps — ta, mate.

Q3 These sentences sound fairly "chatty". Rewrite them so that they are more suitable for inclusion in a piece of written work, using the words in brackets.

   a) He kept changing his mind. (constantly)

   b) Maybe he'll agree. (he may)

   c) No one believed it for a second. (incredible)

   d) Everyone tried very hard to do something about it. (a great effort)

I divn't nah any o' that cockney rhyming slang, like...*

It's fine to use non-standard English when you're chatting or e-mailing friends or whatever. BUT, you have to use standard English in written work — so learn it. Another reason standard English is great is that pretty much everyone in the country will understand it. Dead useful, innit...

* as a taxi driver in Newcastle once said to me.

Levels of Formality

Q1 Write out this letter, filling in the gaps. Choose words or phrases from the pairs below.

Dear Mr Brown,

……. for your letter.
……. sorry to hear that you ……. enjoy your meal.
……. you would have enjoyed something from our à la carte menu.
……. a voucher which will ……. a ……. meal at any of our restaurants.

Yours sincerely,

A. J. Spudwrangler, for Spudwrangler Restaurants.

| I'm sending you / Please find enclosed | Maybe / Perhaps | Thank you / Thanks |
| entitle you to / give you | didn't / did not | I'm / I am | free / complimentary |

Q2 Write out this article in correct standard English:

> When we was children people wasn't allowed to waste anything. We made everything go a right long way — almost everything were rationed, and our Mam would lam us one for throwing away anything what might still have some use to it.
> Food were still rationed and you had to be very inventive with the cooking. We ate everything what were put in front of us. No one ever said they didn't like nothing.
> In them days we didn't have no modern vacuum cleaners and washing machines, like. They were way too expensive for us ordinary folks. We had to work a sight harder to do the housework but you never heard no one complaining. In those days we knew how to clean things proper. We weren't lazy like you young' uns.

Q3 For each of these sentences and paragraphs, write down in what **context** someone might use it — e.g. **conversation**, **texting**, **e-mail**. Then write out each one in correct standard English.

a) Us'll see what us doing later.

b) I was like "Why can't we go in through here?" and he was all "Use the other entrance madam" and getting all hoity-toity.

c) Went white-water rafting on hols in France. Was ace. Got knocked about in boat — whoah, scary. Won't never forget it, specially while still have bruises!

d) UR PRSNT WS GR8 THX

e) Here, that's the one what I lent Joshua before. What's he doing giving it you?

f) Jen, I'll be out until 4 or so. Tell our Steve to phone us and tell us what time he wants picking up. If you two go down the arcades, don't go spending all your allowance. See ya, Mum.

g) Lighten up for a minute will ya, dude? Sheesh.

Section Five — Varieties of English

Other Varieties of English

Q1 Write down the sentences which are TRUE:
  a) Many areas of the UK have their own regional words for some things.
  b) Different jobs and activities also have their own words, senses, and expressions.
  c) It's often — but not always — possible to tell which part of the country someone comes from, by listening to the way that they speak English.
  d) There are historical reasons for the development of regional dialects.
  e) Some words have one meaning in one dialect, and another meaning in another dialect.

Q2 Write down this list of words. Next to each word, write down as many words as you can which mean the same thing. Underline any words which are restricted to certain areas, or which are old-fashioned.
  a) bread roll
  b) path between houses / gardens
  c) mum
  d) dad
  e) freezing cold
  f) grumpy

Q3 Write down all the words or expressions that you know with the same meaning as the words and phrases listed here:
  a) midday meal
  b) Are you going? (= Are you about to go?)
  c) We went everywhere.
  d) Hi!
  e) delighted (= very pleased)
  f) sandwich

Q4 Underline any words or expressions that you wrote down in Q3 which are not used in standard English.

Q5 Write out these sentences, changing them so that they are correct in standard English:
  a) There's too many of us to go in one car.
  b) I done right well.
  c) Not one of these issues are important.
  d) She asked if she could have a lend of his pen.
  e) There's several new books.

Section Five — Varieties of English

Language Change

Words can take on new meanings, or start to be used in different ways.

Q1 Write out these sentences. Beside each one, write another sentence that uses the **bolded** word in a different sense. I've done the first one for you.

a) Can you **take** Ben to school tomorrow? ➡ *My take on the situation is different.*

b) The fete will be held on the school **playing field**.

c) This is the final **text** we'll be studying for the exam.

d) **Scan** the article for the essential information.

e) Jack was off school with a **virus**.

Q2 For each of these words or phrases, write down at least two sentences which illustrate different meanings or uses:

a) hardware d) juggle
b) disc e) wrap… up
c) memory f) on the ground

Q3 Write down each word or phrase, with the type of **TV programme** where you are likely to hear it. (Choose from the list.)

a) makeover American crime thriller
b) mulching Australian soap
c) pro-vitamin DIY show
d) shooter gardening show
e) barbie (=barbecue) advertisement

Q4 It's not just individual words whose meanings change over time. Copy out these words and phrases, and next to each one put the correct grammatical description from the list.

a) **eco**-warrior new prefix
b) **nimby** new compound noun
c) **Do you want to phone a friend**? new catchphrase
d) "You know Jane?" "Yeah — she's **well** clever." new acronym
e) **screensaver** new phrase
f) **move the goalposts** new use of word within sentence

Q5 Read the list of words below, and then do the questions a) to c).

a) Write the words out into two lists, under the headings
   A: no longer used and **B: has a different old meaning**.

b) Write down the meaning of each word in list A.

c) Write down an old meaning of each word in list B.

| whither   fond   nice   charity   wilt   gentle   liege   ozone   behold |

Section Five — Varieties of English

Section Six — Research and Study Skills

Finding and Using Information

Q1 Unscramble the letters below to give the names of six sources of information.

a) ylbrair
b) treetnin
c) eeaioccdpynl
d) noisevielt
e) thero leepop
f) esnppwaer

Q2 From the sources of information in Q1, choose the three most important to you. Explain how they could give you information.

Q3 Read these four definitions:

BLAFF: Fresh fish poached in a clear stock seasoned with strong hot peppers. Traditional in the French Islands.

PASTELITOS: Small meat-filled turnovers baked in a pastry crust.

LOQUAT: Small yellow-orange stoned fruit the size of an apricot with something of the flavour of a peach.

CALLALOO GREENS: The term is used both for the young leaves of the **dasheen** or **taro** plant and for the Oriental pot-herbs known as Chinese spinach. Available in some West Indian shops.

a) Which of these could I use to make a pudding?

b) Which of these is spicy?

c) Which two plants do callaloo greens come from?

"Now rat's a tough meat Angus, you've to cook it reeeeal good"

Don't eat too much blaff — makes your hair explode...
What do you think about research? See, now I'm not that fond of it because it involves **READING** stuff. I prefer a good documentary. Or a sitcom. Or maybe just an advert.

Collecting and Combining Information

Read the following sources:

A (rules in sailing handbook)

> There must be strict rules for wearing safety harnesses:
> - Always on deck at night
> - Always in heavy weather
> - Always by new crew when on foredeck
> - By non-swimmers at all times

B (recording from a documentary about sail training)

> **Skipper:** Look, I don't want any of you guys thinking that not wearing your harness is cool, okay? Look — I'm wearing mine, and I always do. I don't want to have to tell any of your parents that I let you fall overboard and get sucked to death by a basking shark.
>
> **Naz:** But they look really stupid. I'll look like a right idiot in one of them.
>
> **Lucy:** And they're well uncomfortable.
>
> **Skipper:** Yeah I know, but if you don't wear your harnesses you could end up slightly dead okay? I don't care how stupid you look. We can all look stupid and alive together.

C

> 17th September
> somewhere in the Indian Ocean
>
> I'm so glad the weather's got calmer. The last few days have been really scary. The waves have been huge. They've been so tall that the boat slides all the way up them, and then my stomach jumps and I feel sick as we slide back down again. Plus I almost slipped over the side yesterday. Probably would have done too if it wasn't for my harness. Wow. This has been pretty intense.

D Luke says, "I don't care what any of you say. Those harnesses look really daft and there's no way I'm wearing one."

Q1 Say what type of English each source is. Choose from the following: formal written English, informal spoken English, informal written English.

Q2 Each of the sources talks about wearing harnesses in a slightly different way. Say what these are.

e.g. **A** states that harnesses *must* be worn.

Q3 Write a paragraph combining all the information from these sources to persuade Luke why wearing a harness is important.

Hint — you could try and second-guess his reaction. Use sentence starters like "I know they look really stupid, but..."

Section Six — Research and Study Skills

Collecting and Combining Information

Read the following sources:

A) Interview with recently sacked girl:

> "I fainted at work last weekend because I was too hot. Our uniform consists of thick woollen trousers, a long-sleeved shirt and a waistcoat. This is the same for winter and summer. So last week, instead, I came in with a pair of shorts and a strappy top. I was cool enough to work that way, but they sent me home and told me not to bother coming back."

B) Statement on the inside cover of the menu:

> This restaurant hopes to provide a relaxed but formal atmosphere where you may enjoy your meals in a clean, non-smoking environment.

C) Memo from the Managing Director to the Human Resources Manager:

> To: Phillipa Healey, Human Resources Manager
> From: Edwina Spawnson, Managing Director
> Date: 12 June
> Subject: Inappropriate dress
>
> It has come to my attention that staff are dressing in revealing and inappropriate attire. I expect you to take matters in hand and put a stop to the wearing of clothing more suitable for the beach than the workplace. Anyone who has difficulty accepting this may wish to seek employment elsewhere. There may be a heatwave, but our company has its professional image to maintain.

Q1 Do you feel that the girl was justified in her actions? Explain your answer.

Q2 What kind of clientelle do you think the restaurant is trying to attract with the statement in source B?

Q3 How would you describe the *tone* of the memo?

Q4 How could you reach a common solution?

Q5 The management of the restaurant decide to get the opinion of all their staff on the issue of uniform in summer. Design a questionnaire to do this.

Section Six — Research and Study Skills

Making and Using Notes

Q1 Look at these ways of reading to understand, and of making notes.
Tick the methods you use and add two more suggestions of your own.

writing in the margins of your own books
highlighting in different colours
underlining
writing comments on sticky notes

not in textbooks, though, or your teacher will get really mad

copying out key words
copying out topic sentences (the main sentence of a paragraph)
drawing diagrams
drawing a flowchart
drawing a mindmap or spider diagram

recording your spoken notes and ideas onto tape
using IT to change the text into your own version

Q2 Write down the techniques that would work best in each of the situations below:

a) giving a presentation on something of your choice
b) writing notes from something you've read
c) revising for an exam

Q3 *Read the following passage on China in 1989 and Tiananmen Square:*

> China's economic reforms ran into problems during 1988 and 1989. Inflation rose to 30%, and wages lagged well behind prices. Student demonstrations began in Tiananmen Square on 17 April 1989. The students were demanding political reform, democracy and an end to communist party corruption. On 4 May, Zhao Ziyang (Party General Secretary) said that the students' "just demands would be met", and allowed the press to report those demands. This outraged Deng Xiaoping (Party Chairman, ruler of China) and his prime minister, Li Peng.
>
> The demonstrations continued into June, with sometimes as many as 250 000 people occupying the square and surrounding streets. It began to look as though the government had lost control and might soon give way to the demands. Behind the scenes, however, a power struggle was going on between Zhao Ziyang and the hardline Li Peng. Li Peng, with the support of Deng Xiaoping, eventually won. Thousands of troops were brought in, and on 3–4 June, the army, using paratroopers, tanks and infantry, attacked the students, killing between 1500 and 3000 of them. Many student leaders were arrested, tried and executed.
>
> There was worldwide condemnation of the massacres, but Deng and the hardliners were convinced that they had taken the right decision.

a) Write out the main points from the passage.

b) Rewrite the passage in your own words.

c) Make a list of bullet points on cards, as you would to give a presentation.

Section Six — Research and Study Skills

Can You Trust What You Read?

When you do research, always remember that some sources are less trustworthy than others. Don't believe everything you read.

Q1 The words in the box are useful for discussing the reliability of sources. For each of the following sources (a to f), say which word best describes its usefulness if you are looking for facts about Shakespeare and his plays.

> trustworthy   unreliable   irrelevant

- a) someone's own homepage called 'Shakespeare a-go-go'
- b) a cookery book
- c) an encyclopedia
- d) a TV programme about American plays
- e) a movie review which mention's Shakespeare's name
- f) an educational website

Q2 Look at this extract from a holiday brochure. Say what the actual facts about the hotel are.

> This stunning, superb hotel is located just where you'd love it to be. Blue skies look down on a blue sea and the spacious blue pool (3m x 3m), and the exciting minigolf course is accessible to all (open Tuesday 7 - 9 pm). The cosy hotel holds an intimate number of people in its 2500 rooms, and the family-run atmosphere is completed by our special home-style eating opportunities (please bring your own equipment and ingredients). Hurry to book! Things are disappearing fast!

Q3 The list below gives the basic facts about a car for sale. Describe it as persuasively as possible for an advertisement. There will be no photo.

- i) blue
- ii) 4 wheels
- iii) 3 doors
- iv) manual gear change
- v) 1 litre engine
- vi) 2 months' tax
- vii) 9 previous owners
- viii) 15 years old

The truth is NOT out there — it's in here...

Research, research, research... ah the joy of having to go through pages and pages of useless nonsense just to find one tiny scrap of information. Marvellous.

Section Six — Research and Study Skills

Evaluating Your Own Critical Writing

When you finish a piece of work, it's important to check the **spelling**, **punctuation**, **grammar** and **general presentation**.

Q1 Proofread the following passage. There are some spelling and punctuation mistakes in it. Rewrite the passage correctly.

Hint: there are 19 mistakes altogether — some are more obvious than others.

> Ever since the poetry of Chaucer, rhyme has been closely asociated with rythm in English poetry It is also to be found in the early poems and songs of many langages.For most English speakers, the first time they meet it is in the form of nursry rhymes, many of which involve numbers (e.g. "One, two, / Buckle my shoe"). This fact supports the theory that rhyme may have origenated, in primitive religious rites and magic spells. From such early beginnings, poetry has has strong links with music — the earlyest ballads were designed to be sung — and rhyme has been a crucial element in the musicality of poetry. it has also been responsible, in large part, for making poetry memarable.
>
> It often has a more subtle function as well, one witch may not be immediatly apparent. By linking one rhyming word with another, poets may introduce associations which confirm, question, or on occasion deny the literal meaning of their words.
>
> Although the most common rhymes consist of only one or two sylables (e.g. lay / way, dreaming / schemeing), triple and even quadruple rymes are to be found — often in comic verse. A particularly good example is W. S. Gilbert's "I Am the Very Model of a Modern Major-General, with lines such as:
>
>> "I'm very well aquanted too with matters mathe*matical*,
>> I understand equations, both the simple and qua*dratical*."

Q2 Which of the following do you need to think about at the end of an English essay?

  a) Have you answered the question that was asked?
  b) Is your answer well-structured?
  c) Did you need to quote from the text?
  d) Have you used evidence to back up what you say?
  e) If you were asked for it, have you given your opinion?
  f) Have you included the word 'extemporaneous' at least seven times?

What do you mean I can't handle criticism — *sob*...

The best thing about being able to criticise your own work is that there'll be even less for other people to point out. So you can be all smug when your work comes back with no red pen on it.

Section Six — Research and Study Skills

What About the Author?

Q1 Why is it sometimes helpful to know a little about the author of a text? Choose from the options below:

    a)   it can help you to understand their point of view
    b)   it can help to uncover different meanings in a text
    c)   it can help you to identify any places where they might be biased
    d)   all of the above

Q2 These mixed-up words are all useful when discussing what the author tells us, and how we understand it. Unscramble them.

    a)   totthusywrr
    b)   ntotthusywrru
    c)   eejctviob
    d)   tubeescivj
    e)   netwivopi
    f)   aauliroth ceoiv
    g)   sadibe

Q3 Read the two quotes below. How do the two different authors feel about 'community'?

    a)   "I want to do what *I* want to do. Just you wait. One day I'm gonna shake the dust off this crummy old town and travel round the world. I'm gonna go places where nobody knows my name — and nobody wants to stick their nose in my business."

    b)   "When I moved out of the city, it was the best thing I ever did. The sense of community out here is wonderful — everybody watches out for everybody else."

Read the following review of Poe's 'The Tell-Tale Heart':

> **Edgar Allan Poe**
> *The Tell-Tale Heart*
> 'The Tell-Tale Heart' is truly a masterpiece of the macabre — madness and murder in all their gory glory. Let go as you are transported into the dark and twisted world of a psychopathic killer.
> Though not for the faint at heart, this is a must for all you horror buffs out there. You'd have to be *crazy* not to read it. Don't go having nightmares now, children.

Q4 Would you interpret the review differently, depending on who had written it? Say how reliable you would consider the review to be if it had been written by each of the following:

    a)   Poe himself
    b)   an independent book reviewer
    c)   Poe's mum

Section Six — Research and Study Skills

Physical Differences in Presentation

Q1 Match up the different presentation styles in the box with the examples below. Write a paragraph describing each style, concentrating on differences in layout.

recipe   newspaper article   music review   poem   advertisement

A

0% FINANCE. ONLY £59, 666 ON THE ROAD

Finance subject to status and conditions. 0% for first year, rising to 99% thereafter. All monies lent secured against buyer's immortal soul. Eternal damnation as standard.

B

Quingombós Cocidos
STEWED OKRA   (serves 6 to 8)

1½ lb fresh okra
1 oz butter
Large onion, finely chopped
8 medium-sized firm ripe tomatoes peeled, seeded and finely chopped
1½ teaspoons fresh hot chillies, finely chopped
1½ teaspoons finely chopped garlic
1½ teaspoons salt
½ teaspoon freshly ground black pepper

C

Gallon Drunk
Fire Music (*Sweet Nothing*)

   James Johnston is Nick Cave after testosterone shots, taking the Bad Seeds' mode of alternative sleaze away from Berlin cabaret and into reptilian, sharp-suited R&B. While "Fire Music" adds a defiantly retro twist to Gallon Drunk's rock dynamics, Johnston's lyrics can sometimes sound feeble and commonplace when compared with Cave's. ("There is a light that shines / Down into my eyes." Yes Jim, it's called the sun.) This doesn't mean the music isn't expertly, soulfully delivered, taking in gospel ("Things Will Change"), 70s wah-wah funk ("Everything's Alright"), even a Dylan cover ("Series of Dreams").

   It's just that this, their fifth album, is unlikely to raise ver Drunk's critical standing above "reliable".
   Tim Footman

D

SALONIKAN GRAVE

I have watched a thousand days
Push out and crawl into night
Slowly as tortoises.
Now I, too, follow these.
It is fever, and not the fight —
Time, not battle, — that slays.

Rudyard Kipling

E

Hampshire donkey found with gills

The scientific community is today in uproar over the discovery of what has been termed a 'merdonkey' in the sleepy village of Littlefield, West Hampshire.

One of the scientists on the scene had this to say: "The animal appears to have evolved the ability to breathe underwater. It is hard to believe that such a drastic change in the donkey's anatomy is purely natural."

Section Six — Research and Study Skills

The Influence of Readers

Q1 Imagine that a cartoonist loses his / her job for drawing something showing the bad side of a political leader. Write a letter in support of the cartoonist to the editor.

Q2 Imagine that a cartoonist has drawn something that you find very upsetting and offensive. Write a letter of complaint to the newspaper editor.

Q3 Imagine you are a newspaper editor for the Wensleydale Evening Post. You only have room for one more story in tomorrow's edition. Choose the one from the list below that you think will be most relevant to your readers:

    a) Flying pig sighted over Guildford.
    b) Wensleydale Council say 'No' to Jaguar tax.
    c) Roads jammed again by jam jar south of Birmingham.
    d) London home to aliens.
    e) Leopards released into the wild near Swansea.

Read the following extract and then answer the questions below:

"No, I'm sorry," said Maria, "I just don't care."
She shuffled her feet a little then looked away.

Q4 How do you interpret Maria's shuffling and her glancing away? Choose from the following:

    a) a sign that she feels bad about what she said
    b) a sign that she is irritated by the situation
    c) her shoes are too tight
    d) she is indifferent to the whole situation and wishes it would go away

Q5 Can you tell what the above author actually intended?

When we read our imagination fills in the blanks. Everyone's imagination is different, so every reader experiences a text in a different way.

"London home to aliens" — I could've told you that...

I mean, the transport system, the traffic jams, the queues, the muggings, the burglaries — these are all clues. I'll tell you what clinches it for me though — the royal family lives there.

Section Six — Research and Study Skills

Section Seven — Author's Craft

Understanding the Author's Craft

*Comparing two writers on a given theme will show you how their **styles** are different, and also what difference that makes to meaning.*

Q1 Read the two examples of love poetry below, and answer the questions which follow.

1. <u>Never Seek To Tell Thy Love</u>
Never seek to tell thy love,
Love that never told can be;
For the gentle wind does move
Silently, invisibly.

I told my love, I told my love,
I told her all my heart,
Trembling, cold, in ghastly fears -
Ah, she doth depart.

Soon as she was gone from me
A traveller came by
Silently, invisibly -
He took her with a sigh. O, was no deny.

William Blake (1757-1827)

2. <u>The Secret</u>
I loved thee, though I told thee not,
Right earlilly and long,
Thou wert my joy in every spot,
My theme in every song.

And when I saw a stranger face
Where beauty held the claim,
I gave it like a secret grace
The being of thy name.

And all the charms of face or voice
Which I in others see
Are but the recollected choice
Of what I felt for thee.

John Clare (1793-1864)

a) Which of the two poems warns against the consequences of declaring your love?
b) In which of the two poems does the narrator still find other loves?
c) Which poem uses some imagery from nature?
d) Which poem relates an event which happened in the narrator's youth?
e) Which poem is addressed to the person the narrator loves?
f) Which poem has the more uneasy ending?

Q2 Some of the themes in the list below apply to both poems and some to just one of them. Copy out the themes from the box which you think the poems have in common. (You should get five.)

| anxiety | regret | secrecy | dismay | love | betrayal | confession | loss |

Q3 Here's a list of different aspects of style. Explain how each is presented in the two poems.
a) 1st person narrative
b) form (number of verses, number of lines in each)
c) metre (rhythm: beats per line)

Q4 Match up the following explanations to the correct poem:
a) past tense throughout is suitable for admitting a mistake as it distances the narrator from the events described
b) present tense at the start gives the poem the feeling of a proverb, a truth that stands for all time
c) the change to the past tense adds to the sense of regret that mistakes, once made, can never be put right
d) the extra two beats on the last line make it sit uneasily with the rest of the poem, like the uneasiness of his regret, and make it a pessimistic ending
e) addressing an unknown audience, of which the reader is one, helps make the poem feel like a universal truth
f) addressing the loved one helps the poem seem like an intimate confession of error
g) the rhyme scheme changes at the point when the mistake was made, helping it to stand out as significant and increasing the sense that it was wrong

Different Interpretations

*Some texts are **adapted** to different media. You'll have seen many TV programmes and films that actually started their lives as books.*

*Often **changes** are made from the original text.*
Some of these are essential because of the different media.

Q1 Read the opening of this novel, then consider the three film openings that follow. Say which you would choose as a) the closest interpretation of the novel and b) the best opening for a film. Also say which one you liked best. Explain your choices.

> *Georgie was eight when he stole his first car. He didn't even know how to drive — but he learned when a police car arrived on the scene. His mum left home three weeks after his dad left. Then, Georgie, the eldest of six, left too. He didn't want to be lumbered with the job of raising the family. He had far bigger fish to fry — and he was still only twelve.*

i) Black and white rooftop view of a sprawling city in the early evening. Could be anywhere in urban Britain. Out of the quiet hum of the city comes the faint wail of a police siren. Cut to young Georgie, frantically trying to put the car in gear, with older boys on the back seat laughing mockingly.

ii) Glaring colours of cheap seventies-style lino in a nondescript hallway of a terraced house. Definitely somewhere in urban Britain. Cut to the kids' room. Camera ranges around the beds, full of sleeping kids of different ages. Stop panning on an empty bed with rumpled sheets. Off-scene, hear the distant bang of the front door. Cut to a girl of about six, waking up with a fright. Close-up on the look of alarm on her face as she turns to see Georgie's bed empty.

iii) Music: 'London's Burning' by The Clash, played over a sequence showing an older Georgie walking at the head of a gang through an underpass at night. Focus on Georgie's face — confident, determined. Others out of focus behind him. Cut to scene outside 'The Golden Eagle' pub — drunken men in a group getting shown out by friendly landlord. Obviously they have been celebrating. Cut again to Georgie's gang — they all pull bandanas up over their faces. One yell heard over the music and they all break into a run. Cut to the men outside the pub who look up in sudden terror.

*How you interpret a text will depend on what your **focus** is.*

Q2 Match the following areas of focus to the correct opening scene from Q1:
 a) Georgie's poor home life and his lack of family feeling.
 b) What Georgie became.
 c) How Georgie started out.

Q3 Look at the statements below. Write out the ones that you think are true.
 a) There's only one correct way to interpret a text.
 b) Different interpretations are valid in different circumstances.
 c) It doesn't matter if the audience's interpretation is different to that intended.
 d) The number of interpretations that can be realised is limited by external factors such as the cost of production and the choice of media.
 e) My interpretation is as valid as that of the producer, a potential customer or my friend Fred.
 f) I can understand more than one interpretation at a time.
 g) It's useful to be able to understand the intended interpretation so that I can evaluate its success.

Section Seven — Author's Craft

Author's Standpoint

An author can use writing to express his or her views.
These views are known as 'the author's standpoint'.

Q1 Read the following extracts, which all describe the same fictional incident.
For each one, write a one-sentence summary of the standpoint expressed by the author.

a) **"TEEN GANGS RUN RIOT"** Residents of the notorious Argent Estate are today reeling after attacks carried out by gangs of youths last night. A group of thirty teenage boys, masked and hooded, rampaged through the estate's main shopping precinct, defacing property and setting fire to bins. Detective Inspector Bruce Brindler says the gangs that have been terrorising locals for weeks are out of control. "The local community has had enough. This was the last straw."

b) **Argent Estate Report to Council by Enbury District Council Community Housing Officer.** Concern has been repeatedly expressed by residents of the Argent Estate on the lack of facilities provided within the housing complex. Recent behaviour by groups of teenage boys from the estate acts as powerful evidence that their concern is justified.

c) **Police Report re: Argent Estate Breach of the Peace, 12th June 2002.** Twelve teenage boys were apprehended at the Falkirk Road shopping precinct at 2300 hrs on the night in question. They admitted on questioning to having spray-painted graffiti on two shop-front steel shutters, and one admitted responsibility for having thrown a lighted cigarette into a public litter bin, causing some rubbish to emit smoke. Several of the boys are known to the police already for having been involved in similar incidents.

Q2 What methods do the authors use to convey their views? Answer the following questions:

a) Which of the extracts seem to be on the boys' side and which are against them?
b) Choose one of the extracts which is against the boys and write down five examples of loaded / emotive language used in it. Explain the meaning of the words you choose.
c) Extracts a) and c) give contradicting evidence. Write down what this evidence is, and say how the difference affects the meaning of the extracts.
d) Think about who wrote each extract and who they wanted to read it.
Explain how this might affect the way in which the extracts are written.

Understanding an author's standpoint can help you work out what meaning they're trying to get across from their writing. Sometimes the same words can mean completely different things when written by two different people.

Q3 For each statement below write down two different meanings — one from the standpoint of each writer:

a) "The government ought to know."
  i) a government spokesman
  ii) an opposition MP

b) "Kerry has a very individual style."
  i) Kerry's friend
  ii) Kerry's enemy

c) "Animals cannot suffer."
  i) an animal rights supporter
  ii) someone who disagrees with the idea of animal rights

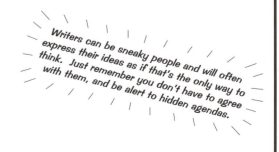
Writers can be sneaky people and will often express their ideas as if that's the only way to think. Just remember you don't have to agree with them, and be alert to hidden agendas.

Section Seven — Author's Craft

Rhetoric

Rhetoric is the name for lots of tricks with words that make your speech or writing persuasive.

Q1 Copy out the following sentences, underlining the parts where you think the author is trying to be persuasive:

- a) How can you allow the poor, suffering little children to go without food for any longer? Send money now.
- b) The Right Honourable gentleman seems to think that everyone has money to spend on whatever they please.
- c) And what is the next step? Struggle, struggle, and still more struggle.
- d) Sybil's interesting; Martha's interesting; Michelle's interesting — just about everybody is interesting in your opinion!
- e) Thank you for coming. We are glad you enjoyed your trip to Dizzyworld. We don't think you'll forget today in a million years!

Q2 Read the list of techniques in the box and match each to the example that uses it in Q1. Each example may use more than one technique.

> i) hyperbole (exaggeration)
> ii) chatty style
> iii) the rule of three (repetition of words / ideas in clumps of 3)
> iv) personal pronouns (using "we" to make speaker and reader part of one group)
> v) playing on the readers' guilt
> vi) criticising the opposite opinion
> vii) repetition of words / phrases for emphasis
> viii) rhetorical questions (ones where the answer is not expected or waited for)
> ix) emotive words (vocabulary chosen for the emotions it conjures up)

When using rhetoric, it's a good idea to make **negative points impersonal** and **positive points personal** to give them maximum impact.

Q3 Say which of the persuasive points below follow the above rule. Answer 'yes' or 'no'.

- a) You've always been useless at thinking ahead — that's why we're in this mess!
- b) We must continue to work for our future.
- c) The world needs to do something about the ecological crisis we face.
- d) It's not just you that has been working hard — everyone in the class has.

Imagine you're about to go on the holiday of a lifetime to Australia and you're trying to persuade your grandad, Bert, to go with you. Thing is, Bert's getting on a bit and has never even left the country before. He can't decide what to do. He'd love to finally have a proper holiday, but at the same time is worried that even if the plane doesn't crash, he'll be eaten by crocodiles.

Q4 Try to persuade Bert to go by writing a persuasive sentence using each of the techniques below. I've done the first one for you.

- a) quote a reliable source ⟹ *e.g. I spoke to Aunty Doris, and she said that you'd love to do something like this.*
- b) use contrasts
- c) use shock tactics
- d) use humour

You visited Dizzyworld — my mate Liz has a season ticket...

She's really cool and all that, but she's absolutely mental. She wears bright clothes and works for Greenpeace. Lovely. But crazy. And no, I don't have anything useful to say about this page.

Section Seven — Author's Craft

Section Eight — Literary Texts

Personal Response

Read this short extract from 'Anne of Green Gables' by Lucy Maud Montgomery:

> It was a pretty good road, running along between snug farmsteads, with now and again a bit of balsamy fir wood to drive through or a hollow where wild plums hung out their filmy bloom. The air was sweet with the breath of many apple orchards and the meadows sloped away in the distance to horizon mists of pearl and purple.

Q1 What impression do we get of the countryside that they are driving through?

Q2 What season do you think it is?

Q3 How does the extract make you feel? Do you like it? Why?

Read the following opening paragraphs of 'The Tell-Tale Heart' by Edgar Allan Poe:

> True! — nervous — very, very dreadfully nervous I had been and am; but why *will* you say that I am mad? The disease had sharpened my senses — not destroyed — not dulled them. Above all was the sense of hearing acute. I heard all things in the heaven and in the earth. I heard many things in hell. How, then, am I mad? Hearken! — and observe how healthily — how calmly I can tell you the whole story.
>
> It is impossible to say how first the idea entered my brain; but once conceived, it haunted me day and night. Object there was none. Passion there was none. I loved the old man. He had never wronged me. He had never given me insult. For his gold I had no desire. I think it was his eye! — yes it was this! He had the eye of a vulture — a pale blue eye, with a film over it. Whenever it fell upon me, my blood ran cold; and so by degrees — very gradually — I made up my mind to take the life of the old man, and thus rid myself of the eye forever.

Q4 How do you feel about the person narrating?

Q5 Read the first paragraph carefully. Do you think the narrator is mad? Say why.

Q6 Look at the second paragraph.
   a) Why does he say he decided to kill the old man?
   b) Apart from the reason in a), did he dislike the old man in any way?

Q7 Do you like this style of writing? Explain why.

Anne of Green Gables is not a slasher movie...
But it should be. Might liven it up a bit. I don't think I've ever read anything so dull in my whole life.

Analysing Drama Texts

Background: Macbeth has won a key battle, has had his future predicted and immediately found one prediction (that he will be made Thane of Cawdor) has come true. In a letter, Macbeth tells his wife about this and about a second prediction that he will be King of Scotland. Lady Macbeth begins to plot King Duncan's murder, but doubts her husband's killing instincts.

Lady Macbeth:	Great Glamis! Worthy Cawdor! Greater than both, by the all-hail hereafter! Thy letters have transported me beyond This ignorant present, and I feel now The future in the instant.
Macbeth:	My dearest love, Duncan comes here tonight.
Lady Macbeth:	And when goes hence?
Macbeth:	Tomorrow, as he purposes.
Lady Macbeth:	O never Shall sun that morrow see! Your face, my thane, is as a book where men May read strange matters. To beguile the time Look like the time; bear welcome in your eye, Your hand, your tongue: look like th'innocent flower But be the serpent under't. He that's coming Must be provided for; and you shall put This night's great business into my dispatch; Which shall to all our nights and days to come Give solely sovereign sway and masterdom.
Macbeth:	We will speak further.
Lady Macbeth:	Only look up clear; To alter favour ever is to fear. Leave all the rest to me.

Q1 What does Lady Macbeth's use of exclamations tell the audience about her state of mind?

Q2 What does Lady Macbeth mean in this quotation: "Thy letters... the instant"?

Q3 What do the repeated instructions, such as "look like" and "leave all the rest to me" tell you about who is in charge in this scene?

Q4 Explain what Lady Macbeth means when she tells Macbeth to "look like th'innocent flower / But be the serpent under't".

Q5 What do you think Macbeth wants his wife to understand when he says "We will speak further"?

Q6 Count up how many words Shakespeare has given to each character. What does this tell you about which is the more powerful in this scene?

Q7 Lady Macbeth greets her husband using his political titles ("Great Glamis! Worthy Cawdor!") while Macbeth greets his wife as his "dearest love". What do these word choices tell the audience about Lady Macbeth and Macbeth's attitudes towards each other, and their concerns?

Section Eight — Literary Texts

Historical Context

Q1 The passage below is taken from 'Persuasion' by Jane Austen:

"You know," said she, "I cannot think him at all a good match for Henrietta; and considering the alliances which the Musgroves have made, she has no right to throw herself away. I do not think any young woman has a right to make a choice that might be disagreeable and inconvenient to the *principal* part of her family, and be giving bad connections to those who have not been used to them. And, pray, who is Charles Hayter? Nothing but a country curate. A most improper match for Miss Musgrove of Uppercross."

a) What does this extract suggest to you about the main purpose of marriage among the privileged classes in Jane Austen's time?

b) What impression do you get about the role of young women in society at that time?

Q2 The following excerpt is from Wilfred Owen's First World War poem 'Dulce Et Decorum Est[1]':

Men marched asleep. Many had lost their boots
But limped on, blood-shod. All went lame; all blind;
Drunk with fatigue; deaf even to the hoots
Of tired, outstripped Five-Nines[2] that dropped behind.

GAS! GAS! Quick, boys! — An ecstasy of fumbling,
Fitting the clumsy helmets just in time;
But someone still was yelling out and stumbling,
And flound'ring like a man in fire or lime...
Dim, through the misty panes and thick green light,
As under a green sea, I saw him drowning.

In all my dreams, before my helpless sight,
He plunges at me, guttering, choking, drowning.

Notes:
1. from the Latin saying: 'Dulce et decorum est pro patria mori' — It is sweet and proper to die for one's country.
2. 5.9-inch calibre shells

a) What does this poem tell you about the **conditions** endured by soldiers during World War One? Use quotes from the text to back up each point you make.

b) How does the author convey his personal feelings about the war?

Hint: look for parts that are written in the first person.

c) The poem ends:

> My friend, you would not tell with such high zest
> To children ardent for some desperate glory,
> The old Lie: Dulce et decorum est
> Pro patria mori.

What does this **suggest** to you about the attitude of society towards war at that time?

d) Why do you think Owen's work is still popular today?

Section Eight — Literary Texts

40

American English

The following extract is part of the opening of 'The Adventures of Huckleberry Finn', which is set in mid-nineteenth century Mississippi in America:

> But Tom Sawyer he hunted me up and said he was going to start a band of robbers, and I might join if I would go back to the widow and be respectable. So I went back.
>
> The widow she cried over me, and called me a poor lost lamb, and she called me a lot of other names, too, but she never meant no harm by it. She put me in them new clothes again, and I couldn't do nothing but sweat and sweat, and feel all cramped up. Well, then, the old thing commenced again. The widow rung a bell for supper, and you had to come to time. When you got to the table you couldn't go right to eating, but you had to wait for the widow to tuck down her head and grumble a little over the victuals*, though there warn't really anything the matter with them, — that is, nothing only everything was cooked by itself. In a barrel of odds and ends it is different; things get mixed up, and the juice kind of swaps around, and the things go better.
>
> After supper she got out her book and learned me about Moses and the Bulrushers, and I was in a sweat to find out all about him; but by and by she let it out that Moses had been dead a considerable long time; so then I didn't care no more about him, because I don't take no stock in dead people.
>
> * victuals — food

Q1 Read the extract **twice** and then rewrite the final paragraph in modern standard English. Pay attention to the words and phrases which you need to change the most.

Q2 Write a short essay about the **language** and **style** of this extract. Use the following points to guide you:
  i) use of sentence structure to give impression of speech
  ii) use of repetition for emphasis
  iii) use of American dialect words and phrases
  iv) how is Huck's character revealed?

American and Standard English — never the Twain shall meet...

American literature's great — it's all spelt wrong. Well, you know what I mean. Mark Twain wrote like that because it was how people talked — so it felt more real. Meanwhile, over here, the Brontë lot were writing novels in really stuffy, old-fashioned Standard English. Pretty dull in comparison.

Section Eight — Literary Texts

Two Ways of Approaching a Theme

Below are two different poems about night:

Windy Nights

Whenever the moon and stars are set,
    Whenever the wind is high,
All night long in the dark and wet,
    A man goes riding by.
Late in the night when the fires are out,
Why does he gallop and gallop about?

Whenever the trees are crying aloud,
    And ships are tossed at sea,
By, on the highway, low and loud,
    By at the gallop goes he.
By at the gallop he goes, and then
By he comes back at the gallop again.

R L Stevenson

Meeting at Night

The grey sea and the long black land;
And the yellow half-moon large and low;
And the startled little waves that leap
In fiery ringlets from their sleep,
As I gain the cove with pushing prow,
And quench its speed i' the slushy sand.

Then a mile of warm sea-scented beach;
A tap at the pane, the quick sharp scratch
And blue spurt of a lighted match,
And a voice less loud, thro' its joys and fears,
Than the two hearts beating each to each!

Robert Browning

Q1 Write in your own words a detailed summary of what each poem is about. You could start like this: *"In 'Windy Nights', the poet begins by setting the scene..."*

Q2 Make up two lists which compare the **similarities** and the **differences** in the details of both poems.

Q3 Choose, from the box below, the word(s) which best describe the **atmosphere** or **mood** of each poem, and give reasons for your answer.

> mysterious   romantic   dramatic   haunting   ghostly   frightening   secretive
> dangerous   urgent   enigmatic (look it up in the dictionary)

Q4 Write down two or three quotations from each poem which contribute to its mood. Give reasons for your choices, e.g.

In 'Meeting at Night' you could argue that "two hearts beating each to each" is romantic because we associate hearts with love.

Q5 Find examples of repetition in both poems.

Q6 In both poems the poets raise questions in your mind which are never fully answered.
Write three questions you would like to ask about each poem, e.g.

In 'Windy Nights', is the man a ghost?

Q7 Write a short essay about the differences and similarities you have found in the way that these two poets deal with the theme of 'night'. Use your earlier answers to help you. Finish by saying which poem you prefer, giving reasons for your choice.

Section Eight — Literary Texts

Analysing Powerful Writing

The following extract is adapted from the end of the first chapter of Charles Dickens' novel, 'Great Expectations'. Pip, a young boy, is threatened in a churchyard by a convict, desperate for food and a tool to cut the chains from his leg.

> I said that I would get him the file, and I would get him what broken bits of food I could, and I would come to him at the Battery, early in the morning.
>
> 'Say Lord strike you dead if you don't!' said the man.
>
> At the same time, he <u>hugged</u> his shuddering body in both his arms — <u>clasping</u> himself, as if to hold himself together — and <u>limped</u> towards the low church wall. As I saw him go, picking his way among the nettles, and among the brambles that bound the green mounds, he looked in my young eyes as if he were eluding the hands of the dead people, stretching up cautiously out of their graves, to get a twist upon his ankle and pull him in.
>
> When he came to the low church wall, he got over it, like a man whose legs were numbed and stiff, and then turned round to look for me. When I saw him turning, I set my face towards home, and made the best use of my legs. But presently I looked over my shoulder, and saw him going on again towards the river, still hugging himself in both arms, and <u>picking</u> his way with his sore feet among the great stones dropped into the marshes here and there, for stepping-places when the rains were heavy, or the tide was in.
>
> The marshes were just a long black horizontal line then, as I stopped to look after him; and the river was just another horizontal line, not nearly so broad nor yet so black; and the sky was just a row of long angry red lines and dense black lines intermixed. On the edge of the river I could faintly make out the only two black things in all the prospect that seemed to be standing upright; one of these was the beacon by which the sailors steered — like an unhooped cask upon a pole — an ugly thing when you were near it; the other a gibbet*, with some chains hanging to it which had once held a pirate. The man was limping on towards this latter, as if he were the pirate come to life, and come down, and going back to hook himself up again. It gave me a terrible turn when I thought so; and as I saw the cattle lifting their heads to gaze after him, I wondered whether they thought so too. I looked all round, and could see no one else. But, now I was frightened again, and ran home without stopping.
>
> * *gibbet* — a scaffold used for hanging criminals

Q1 Analyse the author's use of language in describing the convict. Use the questions below to help you:

  a) What impression of the man's situation and state of mind is created by the underlined verbs?

  b) What other details does the author use to suggest the man's terrible situation?

  c) What is the effect of the repetition of the word 'black' in the last paragraph?

Q2 What different methods does the author use to suggest that Pip is a very young child?

Q3 Who do you think the author wants us to think is the more frightened of the two characters — the narrator or the escaped convict? Give reasons for your answer.

Q4 Imagine the film of this part of the book, and describe what the audience would see and hear if you were the director. Justify your ideas by close reference to the text.

Q5 The extract gives Pip's point of view. Rewrite it from the point of view of the escaped convict, making clear his state of mind and his attitude toward the young narrator.

Section Eight — Literary Texts

Section Nine — Essay Skills

Different Styles

You have to be able to change your writing style for different purposes and audiences.

Q1 Write down what **style** each of these sentences is written in.
Choose from the options in the box below.

a) 14th June — We left the shelter for the first time today and surveyed the damage — the storm had levelled the site. It was a real mess.

b) Insert the optical cable into the socket marked **digital output**.

c) The sun sets silent,
over the snowcapped mountain.
Red to black — night falls.

d) The city is, this week, buzzing with excitement as the big day approaches — the atmosphere out on the streets is electric.

e) Dear Sarah, Sorry I've not been in touch for a while — I've been so busy with exams and stuff. So, how's everything going honey?

f) 3. a) It is the responsibility of you, the tenant, to report any damage to the property, accidental or otherwise, to the landlord within 48 hours.

> letter   newspaper report   legal document
> journal / diary   instruction manual   poem

Think about your audience.

Q2 Imagine that you've just returned from a month of watching gorillas in their natural habitat. Write down the best style to use to write about your experience for each of the following:

a) a close friend
b) a wildlife magazine
c) someone about to take the same trip as you, for the first time

Q3 Read the following eyewitness account. Write about the event it describes in each of the styles below, a) to c).

> "It was last Saturday. I was sat at a table outside my favourite coffee shop having breakfast. There was no one else around — it must have only been about eight o'clock.
> A young couple came and sat on a bench across the road. They seemed to argue about something, but I can't be sure. A big car with blackened windows pulled up in front of them and someone got out. He (at least, I'm assuming it was a 'he') was wearing a long black trenchcoat, a wide-brimmed hat, and had a scarf wrapped round the bottom of his face. He talked to the young man for a while and they seemed to come to some kind of agreement. Two thugs got out, grabbed the girl, and threw her kicking and screaming into the back of the car. The two men shook hands. Trenchcoat-guy got back in the car and drove off. The young man sat down like nothing had happened, and I rang the police."

a) newspaper report
b) a spy / crime / science-fiction story
c) letter to a friend

Writing an Article

Read the following passage:

> There's all these big scary white ducks up by the golf course with bright red beaks and they run at you quacking and try and nick your lunch and last week one of them disappeared. Everyone reckoned a fox had had it. People had seen a fox around, and foxes like to eat ducks, apparently. Everyone was a bit upset about it really. Anyway, I reckoned there might be something a bit fishy about the whole business. I decided to go and have a word with these people who'd seen the 'fox'. They said they'd seen it hanging around for a few days before the duck disappeared. I reckoned this was a bit weird as well 'cause if the fox wanted a duck, why didn't it just take it? It had to be a set-up — someone was trying to blacken the fox's name, and I wasn't going to stand for it. I went into Miss Marple mode, and went to track down the real culprit. I looked back at the scene of the crime and there were these big scatches in the ground, you know, the sort that might have been made by a bird, but the ducks don't have talons like that on their feet, they're all big and flat and webbed and stuff. It looked like a chicken had made them, and it's common knowledge that the local chickens have got this thing about the ducks. There's this big rivalry thing going on. I went down to the farm to have a snoop around but the chickens were being very tight-beaked about the whole situation, and one of them was missing. I decided to hang around outside for a while and lo and behold, as I was sat there watching the door to the coop, she showed up carrying a big bundle in her beak. I stepped up and grabbed it. It was a fox costume! I'd found my culprit, but by then she'd done a runner.

Q1 Summarise the passage in 20 words or less.

Work out what's not important.

Q2 Make a bullet point list of all the facts in this passage that could be used to write a newspaper article.

Q3 Which of the following would be the best headline for the story? Explain what's wrong with each of the others.
- a) Fox Frenzy in Golf Course Murder
- b) Chicken Snatcher Still at Large
- c) Foxy Chick in Duck-Snatching Shocker
- d) "Duck" Says Chicken with Gun

Q4 Write the article. Include the following things:
- a) concise introduction
- b) precise telling of the facts (no waffling)
- c) punchy conclusion

Weirdest page in book — we apologise for the inconvenience...

Yes, erm, sorry about this page. It is a bit random. Then again, loads of them are. Could be worse. Could have made a joke about goats. Oops. Sorry. I mentioned the "G" word.

Section Nine — Essay Skills

Formal Essays

Q1
> The smell their drummer made onstage really put us off the gig. I told him we wouldn't bother seeing them again. In fact, I told them they could naff off. They used to be my favourite band, but they're not now — they haven't been since last year.

Say which of the following statements apply to the above passage:
a) There is no introduction.
b) It doesn't explain who the band are, or give any other context.
c) It just trails off without a conclusion.
d) The grammar and punctuation are atrocious.

Q2 Say which of the following sentences could be included in a formal essay about someone's favourite band:

a) My favourite heavy metal band, "Orange Hamster" (formed in 1977), are as popular today as they ever were.

b) The O' Hamster have been kicking around for about 25 years now, and they're still packing them in at every gig.

c) "Grannyknot" suck — they can't play and their lead singer's a muppet.

d) "Grannyknot" are a band that I strongly dislike. They have very little musical talent, and their lead singer is painfully middle-of-the-road.

e) My favourite musical genre is 60s rhythm and blues.

f) The best stuff around is old-time R&B.

Q3 Give yourself 5 minutes to write down a bullet point list about what music you like and dislike, favourite bands, etc.

Q4 Now give yourself 15 minutes (time yourself) to write a formal mini-essay about your own musical tastes. Include your favourite band and favourite song (or songs). The essay should be about 200 words long, and should include an introduction and a conclusion.

Section Nine — Essay Skills

Formal Letters

Read this postcard:

> Hi Andy,
> You wouldn't believe what Miss Cookridge has got us doing now. A sponsored silence to pay for new books for the school library! Twenty-four hours of SILENCE, me! It's going to drive me mad (don't say it). Anyway, she wants us to write this big formal letter thing to send to everyone in the neighbourhood. They're all mean up our way too, so I probably won't even get sponsored. Anyway, I'll be in touch again soon Honey. Love Jules xx

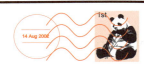

Andrea Kiernan
25 Street Lane
Littleton
Cumbria

Q1 Imagine that you are Jules. Write the formal letter asking for sponsorship. Your letter should include:

a) your address at the top of the page (you can make one up if you want)
b) the date
c) formal salutation (i.e. Dear Sir / Madam,)
d) opening paragraph explaining clearly **who** you are and **what** you are asking for
e) details about the cause
f) when you will visit them
g) closing sentence
   e.g. The school thanks you for any contribution you wish to make.
h) sign off with 'Yours faithfully'

Q2 Your Granny has a bad experience in a department store. She tells you what happened:

> "Oooh you won't believe what 'appened to me, you won't. I went into 'Marks and Spinster' to get myself some new thick woollen tights, only they'd run out. So I asked the little girl behind the counter if they was getting any more in and she laughed at me and called me an old bag. In my day children was seen and not 'eard, and she can't 'ave been more than about 16 and she 'ad a right mouth on her. I've never heard anything like it in my life. That's the last time I shops for tights in 'Marks and Spinster', that's for bloomin' well certain."

Your granny asks you to write a formal letter of complaint for her. Your opening paragraph should summarise her complaint and your final paragraph should suggest a solution. Make sure that you use suitably formal language.

I like woollen tights — they make me feel all warm inside...

Writing letters is a pain in the neck, but they'll help you all your life. They can help you get a job or, in my case, they can help explain to the pet shop where you got the goat from in the first place.

Section Nine — Essay Skills

Section Ten — Writing Fiction

Writing Stories

*There are many different **genres** (types) of story. For example, action or romance. In your story writing you need to make your readers aware of the genre you are using.*

Q1 The following sentences are each taken from a different genre of story. Match up the sentences with the correct genre from the box.

- a) The sounds of the exploding bullets ricochet around the battlefield.
- b) It took some time to find the body. The woods in which it was buried were overgrown, forbidding and remote.
- c) "Blast off!" The power of the engines vibrated through the astronaut's body.
- d) Richard Cragg strapped on his boots with determination. This was going to be the hardest climb of his life.
- e) The sun set sending its golden rays across the bay, silhouetting two figures, hand in hand on the water's edge.
- f) Terrence the tortoise was always having adventures. Today was no exception.
- g) Wolves howled, bats shrieked. By the light of the full moon the vampires met to feast.

> science fiction
> romance
> horror
> war
> mystery / crime
> action
> animal stories

Q2 Choose any **three** of the above genres and write your own opening sentences to a story. Make sure that they make the genre clear and would interest your reader.

A sentence can often be written in different ways, but still have the same meaning. It is important to word the first sentence of your story in a way which will grab the reader's attention.

Q3 Rewrite the following sentences in at least two different ways. I've done the first one for you.

- a) The woman slowly opened the door to the dark cellar.
- a) *Slowly the woman opened the door to the dark cellar.*
  The door to the dark cellar was slowly opened by the woman.
- b) The soldiers cowered in the damp trenches, fear written all over their faces.
- c) The spaceship hurtled towards the burning planet, spinning out of control.
- d) Nervously, the young man approached the beautiful model.
- e) She glanced behind her into the shadows, convinced she heard footsteps.
- f) Tired after his adventures, Terrence retreated into his shell.
- g) Roaring like an express train, the snow charged down the mountainside towards the stricken climbers.

I've got loads of books — they're piled ten stories high...*

It's important to make the start of your story <u>top notch</u>, whatever genre you're writing in. If the reader isn't interested right from the start, then they'll never get as far as the dramatic shipwreck, violent double murder and long awaited marriage of Cyril to Betty in the last chapter. Try writing and rewriting your opening sentences until you're happy with them.

* no that's not how you're meant to spell it.

Writing Stories

*Once you've got your story started, you need to know where to go next. You'll know that a story should have a beginning, a middle and an end. But story writing can also be split up into **six** different stages.*

Q1 Put the following six stages of a story into the correct order:

a) complication
b) resolution
c) introduction
d) adjustment
e) introduce a problem
f) crisis

Q2 Match up the following sentences to the six stages in Q1.
Copy out the sentences in the correct order to give an outline for the story.

a) She found food and a place to rest before she went home.
b) It was a beautiful sunny day, so Goldilocks decided to go for a walk.
c) She found a cottage, but no one was home so she let herself in.
d) She fell asleep and the owners of the house, three bears, came home and discovered her.
e) Goldilocks woke up just in time and ran away before the bears could eat her.
f) She walked so far she got lost and was very hungry.

Most fairy tales end in unimaginative ways, e.g. "...they all lived happily ever after."

Q3 Match the following poor endings with their more interesting alternatives from the box:

a) They all lived happily ever after.
b) The alarm clock sounded. It was all a dream.
c) The butler did it.
d) They were together again at last.
e) They were all dead.
f) They sailed off into the sunset.
g) I was so glad that the evil monster was dead.

The butter did it. Get it?.. the butter... Nobody appreciates my comedy genius.

Not a hair flickered on the slaughtered bodies as they lay scattered on the bloody field.
The alarm clock sounded. It was the 7th of September, all over again!
They were together again at last, but for how long?
"You will never defeat me!" cackled the vampire.
The boat, silhouetted against the sunset, carried the two lovers to their destiny.
Life returned to normal, until the next time.
At last they had found the serial killer, but had they found all the victims?

Q4 Look back to the three stories you started on p47 (Q2), and write a last sentence for them. Try to leave your reader with some unanswered questions.

Section Ten — Writing Fiction

Adding Description

Adjectives are descriptive words. Choosing the right ones is important in making your writing interesting.

Q1 Underline all the adjectives in the following passage:

> A glorious day had begun. The powder-blue sky was dotted with cotton-wool clouds. A swallow flitted through the still air, her sharp wings slicing a path effortlessly. Her turns were swift and precise; she was supreme. Below her on the tiny country lanes, red-faced humans crawled along in their metal coffins, sweating and sighing their way to the crowded beaches.

You can change the mood of a piece completely by choosing different adjectives.

Q2 Copy out the piece above, changing the adjectives to show that the swallow is small and that the humans are powerful. You may have to change some other words too.

The English language often contains many words for the same thing. This means you can express tiny differences between ideas by just changing a word.

Q3 Match up the following words with their synonyms (words that can have the same meaning) from the box:

a) big
b) small
c) old
d) young
e) new
f) good
g) nice
h) horrible

new-born	useful
pleasant	minute
huge	ancient
awful	recent

Q4 Write down three more synonyms for each of the words in the box above.

Hint: a thesaurus is a good place to look for ideas.

Another way of making your writing interesting is to try to put pictures in the mind of your reader by reminding them of something else.

Similes make comparisons between two objects by using '**like**' or '**as**'.

Q5 Complete the following similes with the animal names from the box:

a) like a ... in a china shop
b) as slow as a ...
c) as sly as a ...
d) like a faithful ...
e) as stubborn as a ...
f) like a curious ...
g) as strong as an ...
h) like a ... out of water

| ox fox fish cat |
| dog bull snail mule |

Section Ten — Writing Fiction

Other Types of Entertaining Writing

Now that you know how to make stories interesting, it's time to look at advertising slogans. An entertaining slogan will encourage more people to buy the product.

Q1 Imagine you've designed a new soft drink, a new car and a new chocolate bar. Write down your own slogans to advertise them. Make them as entertaining as you can.

Q2 Some slogans use techniques that fiction writers use too. Match up each definition with the correct term from the box:

    a) A play on words, where one word has more than one meaning.
    b) Repetition of the initial sound in two or more words that are close together.
    c) They tell the reader to do something.
    d) Asks your reader a question that requires no answer.
    e) Words that describe.

> alliteration
> adjectives
> pun
> commands
> rhetorical question

Q3 Look back at the slogans you wrote for Q1. Did you use any of the above techniques? Have another go. This time use three of the techniques from the box.

Advertising slogans aren't the only examples of non-fiction which use entertaining language. Newspapers do too, especially puns.

Q4 Copy out these headlines, filling in the missing words from the box.

    a) A RIGHT PAIR OF …
    Two thieves were arrested last night, trying to break into an underwear factory.

    b) FIRE BREAKS OUT AT … PALACE
    David Beckham was unhurt last night after a small fire in his mansion.

    c) … FOR OPTIMISM?
    Discussions have taken place about ground-sharing to save smaller football clubs.

    d) TOO COLD TO … ALL ON …
    Cool weather means sunbathers on Britain's beaches need to wrap up.

    e) BATON … FOR BARBARA
    Young sports star chosen for national relay competition.

    f) THE … TO EAT!
    New fish and chip shop opens in town.

> Beckingham
> plaice
> knickers
> grounds
> bare
> beckons
> beaches

Section Ten — Writing Fiction

Different Types of Poetry

*Poetry is another form of writing designed to imagine, explore or entertain. Poets have to choose their words carefully, just like other writers. They also need to think about the **structure**, **rhythm** and **rhyme** of their poems. This is called the **form**.*

Q1 Copy out the following verses of poetry. They all have a line missing. Choose a line from the box to complete each verse.

a) The Owl and the Pussy-Cat went to sea
In a beautiful pea-green boat.
They took some honey, and plenty of money,
....

b) Round, golden and warm
Gives life to all who dwell there
....

c) There was an old man from Crewe
Who found he had nothing to do
So he sat on the stairs,
And counted his hairs
....

d) Tyger! Tyger! Burning bright,
....
What immortal hand or eye,
Could frame thy fearful symmetry?

e) Two households, both alike in dignity
In fair Verona, where we lay our scene
From ancient grudge break to new mutiny
....

> Where civil blood makes civil hands unclean
> Glorious, the sun.
> In the forests of the night,
> And found that he only had two.
> Wrapped up in a five-pound note.

To work out the rhyme scheme of a poem call the first line A. Every line that rhymes with it is also A. The next line that doesn't rhyme is B and so is every line that rhymes with it. And so on ...

Q2 The above verses are examples of different forms of poetry.
Copy out the definitions below and match them to the correct example from Q1.

a) A <u>limerick</u> has five lines. The first two rhyme together, the third and fourth lines rhyme with each other, and the fifth line rhymes with the first two, (AABBA).

b) A <u>sonnet</u> is a fourteen-line poem with ten syllables in each line. There are different rhyme schemes for different types of sonnet.

c) A <u>haiku</u> is a three-line Japanese poem. The first and last lines have five syllables each, and the middle line has seven syllables.

d) An example of a <u>regular rhyming scheme</u> is when every other line rhymes. This pattern goes all the way through the poem (often like ABAB CDCD etc.).

e) Another example of a regular rhyming scheme is <u>rhyming couplets</u>. This is when pairs of lines rhyme together.

Q3 Choose three of the forms above and write your own poems.
For example, you could try writing a haiku, a limerick and a sonnet on the same subject.

There was a young witch called Heather,
Who was small and light as a feather.
Many spells she could do,
And lots of potions she knew;
She could even predict the weather.

Poets are people too — aww...

Well there's a little limerick for you. I'm quite proud of it really — I've got the rhyme scheme right and everything. You could even use it for Q3 if you're desperate... really, really desperate...

Section Ten — Writing Fiction

Section Eleven — Writing Information

Writing Coherent Accounts

Any writing to inform needs to be clear and precise.

Q1 Say which of the following sentences give information clearly.
a) Rap music originated in the cities of America.
b) It was written by someone a long time ago so the words are different.
c) There are more people in China learning English as their second language than there are people in the whole of America.
d) World War II lasted six years, from 1939 till 1945.
e) It takes a long time and you get really tired.
f) They play in white shirts when they are at home and use red shirts when they play somewhere else.
g) It goes really high and you can see right across there.

Q2 Rewrite the sentences from Q1 that are too vague. The box below says what each one is meant to be about. Make sure you match the right sentence to the right subject.

> one is about 'Romeo and Juliet' by Shakespeare
> one is about the London Eye
> one is about the England football team
> one is about running a marathon

Sentences like those you wrote in Q2 are called topic sentences. They begin paragraphs and make it very clear what that paragraph will be about.

Q3 Copy out the sentences below, completing them with a word (or words) from the box:
a) Louis Armstrong was a famous ....
b) .... is partly caused by pollution from coal-burning power stations.
c) The .... is a collection of countries ruled by the British Queen.
d) The phrase '....................' came from a book by George Orwell.
e) .... is important to stay healthy.
f) Neil Armstrong was a famous .... and was the first man on the moon.

> acid rain   Olympic Games   Big Brother   musician
> Commonwealth   regular exercise   astronaut

Q4 The following sentences lead on from two of the topic sentences in Q3. Copy them out under the relevant topic sentence.
a) He was part of the Apollo 11 mission by NASA.
b) Emissions from car exhausts also cause problems.
c) On a later mission to the moon, the astronauts played golf.
d) When acid rain falls, it damages trees and pollutes rivers.
e) Even today, three decades later, there are still golf balls on the moon.
f) In some countries, lakes are so polluted that local people can no longer fish or swim there.

Q5 You now have two model paragraphs that give information. Write your own paragraph to inform, based on a subject you know a lot about. Remember to use a topic sentence.

Writing Coherent Accounts

> *Modal verbs* (may, should, have, can, etc.) are often used in writing to inform because they express small differences between ideas and help you to be precise and clear.
>
> Modal verbs 'help out' the main verb. They have no meaning by themselves but are very useful partners to other verbs.

should	must	could

Q1 Complete the sentences below using one of the modal verbs from the box above. The sentences in *italics* tell you what precise meaning you need to give.

a) We lost the match but we ………… have won.
We were the better team. The result wasn't fair.

b) We lost the match but we ………… have won.
Both teams had the chance to win.

c) He ………… hurry or he'll miss his meeting.
His meeting is very important.

d) Sarah walked right past me — she ………… have seen me.
You were wearing a bright orange T-shirt that reads "I am here".

e) Sarah walked right past me — she ………… have seen me.
You think there's a chance that Sarah saw you.

Of course, modal verbs can be negative too.

might not	will not (won't)	should not	must not

Q2 Copy and complete these sentences with one of the negative modal verbs from the box above. (Use each one once.)

a) It's been raining most of the day. We ………. be able to have our barbecue.

b) You ………. try to find me. If you do, I will cut out your heart with a spoon.

c) That's it. We've got a flat tyre. We ………. be going anywhere today.

d) You ………. have come over. This bouncy castle isn't big enough for the both of us.

Q3 Write six sentences of your own, each using the modal verb suggested below:

a) must   d) might not
b) won't   e) should
c) could   f) must not

I might write something funny now — or I might not...

Other modal verbs that sometimes get used are: <u>may</u> or <u>may not</u>, <u>have to</u> or <u>have not</u>, <u>ought</u> or <u>ought not</u>. I really <u>ought to</u> leave off and go home now, or I <u>might</u> regret it. Also, I'm bored.

Section Eleven — Writing Information

Connecting Ideas

Connectives are words that make the links between your ideas very clear. Connectives (words like so, because, although, until, etc.) are useful in writing to inform because your writing becomes easier to follow.

Q1 Copy out the sentences below, underlining the connectives.

   a) It is important to drive slowly past schools because children may be playing nearby.
   b) My gran enjoys pop music even though she is really old.
   c) My cat never wakes up unless he is hungry.
   d) We went for a picnic despite the rain.
   e) I was really tired so I went to bed early.
   f) My teacher told me I'd be in detention unless I stopped talking.
   g) The shops were all shut as it was a public holiday.

Connectives do not have to go in the middle of the sentence. You can keep your writing varied by using connectives at the start of sentences.

Q2 Rewrite the sentences from Q1, moving the connective to the beginning. I've done the first one for you as an example.

   a) *Because children may be playing nearby, it is important to drive slowly past schools.*

Choosing the wrong connective can change the meaning of your sentence. It's really important to be precise.

Q3 Each of the following sentences has been written using the wrong connective. Rewrite the sentences using a better one.

   a) David Beckham lives in Hertfordshire **because** he plays in Manchester.
   b) The fire-eater had a day off work **even though** he had a sore throat.
   c) Pollution will not decrease **so** people use their cars less.
   d) English weather is unpredictable **because** we go on holiday to Florida.
   e) He was easy to understand **because** he started speaking a language I had never heard.
   f) **Until** I had broken my leg, I couldn't take part in Sports Day.

Q4 Write sentences of your own, using each of the connectives below:

   a) because
   b) so
   c) even though
   d) until
   e) despite
   f) as

I am the God of Hellfire — bring me a lozenge...

Connecting words need to be used wisely, or else you just end up with a whole lot of short sentences. Like this one. Or this one. Maybe this. This. Yep. *sigh*

Section Eleven — Writing Information

Using Descriptive Detail

There are many different kinds of informative writing. As well as giving information, sometimes you need to paint a picture for your reader too.

Q1 Copy out the travel journal below and underline all the sentences or phrases that just give information. Use a different colour to underline the sentences or phrases that help paint a picture for the reader.

> It's hard to believe that Bangkok is a capital city. It's a crazy collection of tranquil wats (temples) and manic markets, noisy taxis and fantastic food stalls. The most common sight though is a temple. Many people in Bangkok are Buddhists and there are temples on every street. Beautiful statues, quiet courtyards and gentle fountains can be found in every temple. If you go into one of these beautiful places, remember to remove your shoes as a sign of respect.

Look back at the passage from Q1. Without the detail to paint a picture it would be quite boring to read.

Q2 Copy out the sentences below (a to g). Match up each information sentence with one from the box that adds more detail.

- a) It was the 93rd minute of the match when the referee gave a free kick.
- b) Barcelona is an important city in Spain because of its architecture.
- c) The favourite for the 100 m was already Olympic champion.
- d) The tennis match went to five sets.
- e) It was 3.30 when I saw the robber come out of the bank.
- f) Alton Towers is one of the most popular places in Britain for a day out.
- g) I saw him get into a black car minutes later.

- i) He was supremely fit, exceptionally strong and completely confident: he knew the gold medal belonged to him.
- ii) He seemed really nervous and kept glancing behind him like a rabbit being chased by a fox.
- iii) The captain stepped up confidently and placed the ball precisely, brushing aside his anxious team-mates who told him who to pass the ball to.
- iv) With wheels squealing, it sped away followed closely by a police car, siren screaming.
- v) After two nail-biting hours, the Wimbledon champion would soon be known.
- vi) Magnificent church spires, impressive mansions and modern skyscrapers fill the horizon of this city, a mix of old and new.
- vii) Crowds flock here every summer, anxious to try out the latest death-defying roller coasters.

Q3 The sentences in Q2 all come from sports reports, travel writing or eyewitness accounts. Choose one of the sentences and use it as the starting point to write a paragraph of sport or travel writing.

Section Eleven — Writing Information

Text Layout

*When you are writing to inform, the way you present your writing is important.
You can choose to lay out your writing in a number of ways.*

Q1 Match up each **presentational device** below with the correct description.

headline	strapline	caption
subheading	bullet points	illustrations

a) a short line of writing under a photo, giving some extra detail about the picture

b) a way of listing information, separating each piece of information

c) a kind of title that goes above the writing and catches the reader's attention

d) pictures, graphs, photos, cartoons which make texts more interesting to look at

e) one or two words, like mini-titles, that break up the main text into smaller chunks

f) a line of writing under a headline, adding detail to the headline

Q2 Look at the text below. Name the different layout styles used:

Hint: think about how each bit is different in terms of size and appearance.

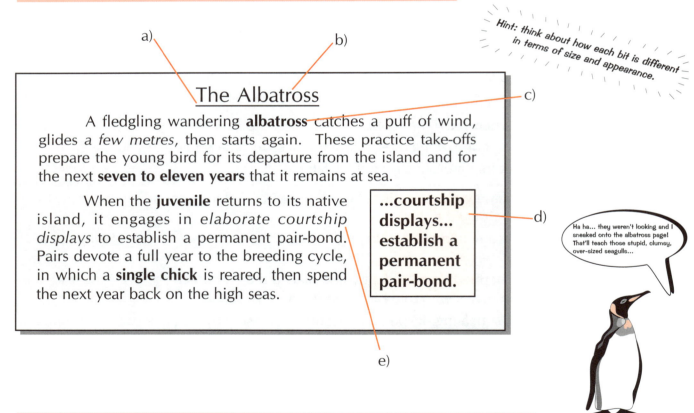

The Albatross

A fledgling wandering **albatross** catches a puff of wind, glides *a few metres*, then starts again. These practice take-offs prepare the young bird for its departure from the island and for the next **seven to eleven years** that it remains at sea.

When the **juvenile** returns to its native island, it engages in *elaborate courtship displays* to establish a permanent pair-bond. Pairs devote a full year to the breeding cycle, in which a **single chick** is reared, then spend the next year back on the high seas.

...courtship displays... establish a permanent pair-bond.

Ha ha... they weren't looking and I sneaked onto the albatross page! That'll teach those stupid, clumsy, over-sized seagulls...

Q3 Look back at your sports or travel report from page 55. Use some of the presentational devices above to turn your report into a newspaper article.

Journalists are great — unless you're famous...

There really is an art to writing for a newspaper. Journalists aren't just annoying people who don't give anyone any privacy... they're talented writers who know how to get a reaction. Of course that doesn't mean they're *not* annoying, I'm just saying like...

Section Eleven — Writing Information

Section Twelve — Writing to Persuade

Using Adjectives

Writing to persuade is like trying to influence people in conversation. It's vital to grab their attention.

Q1 Copy out these sentences, underlining the words that grab your attention:

- a) Animal testing is pointless, cruel and heartless.
- b) School uniform is constricting, unfashionable and costly.
- c) Action films are always exciting, explosive and thrilling.
- d) No one should be forced to wear clothes they detest.
- e) Animal testing is vital for human survival.
- f) Football is definitely the most popular sport in the world.
- g) We all get a sense of pride by wearing our school uniform.
- h) Animals share this planet with us.
- i) Everyone should make an effort to recycle.

Using three adjectives is a powerful way to persuade.

Q2 Complete the following sentences, choosing adjectives from the box below. Use each adjective once only.

- a) Some pupils think that homework is time-consuming, pointless and ....
- b) However, teachers believe that homework is essential, educational and ....
- c) My gran thinks that pop music is loud, ... and ....
- d) Other people believe pop music is entertaining, ... and ....
- e) Sporty people argue that PE is ...., ... and ....
- f) Couch potatoes, however, argue that PE is ...., ... and ....
- g) Rugby can be ...., ... and ....
- h) The British countryside is ...., ... and ....

tuneless	lush	rough	beneficial	tiring	healthy
hard-hitting	invigorating	tedious	rhythmical	peaceful	overrated
funky	bruising	breathtaking	embarrassing	enjoyable	useless

Q3 Write a sentence using any three adjectives on a subject you feel strongly about.

In order to persuade your reader it is important to include them in your point of view.

Q4 Rewrite these sentences to include your reader in your argument. I've done the first one for you.

- a) Whenever I feel ill I want to know that the medicine I take is safe.
  We all want to take medicine that will not harm us.
- b) I would not wish my hamster to be experimented on.
  None of us would...
- c) I hate wearing school uniform because I look like everyone else.
- d) School uniform is good because I am wearing the same as everyone else.
- e) I wish my school uniform was trendier.
- f) I believe that the age rating on films is often wrong.
- g) I know that I would like more facilities where I live.

Hint: don't use 'I', or it just sounds like one person's opinion.

Structuring an Argument

Arguments between people often get out of control. You don't want the same thing to happen to your writing, so make sure your arguments follow a set structure.

Q1 Put these stages of an argument in the correct order:

- a) develop your idea
- b) make a point
- c) introduce your topic
- d) give the opposite view
- e) conclude your argument
- f) give evidence

Q2 These sentences (a to f) are examples of the above stages. Put them in order to form an argument about pop music.

- a) If you want proof, just watch any popular music programme to see how few groups perform live.
- b) The face of music as we know it is changing.
- c) Some people might argue that their favourite band can sing and play instruments, but these bands find it hard to get money from recording companies.
- d) The music charts are full of manufactured pop groups who have been put together to look good.
- e) In conclusion, success in pop music is less about talent and more about good looks, good advertising and good luck.
- f) There are too many groups who cannot play a single instrument or sing live. Their songs are often written for them.

Rhetorical questions make people think but do not need an answer.
Statements can become more interesting and forceful if changed into a rhetorical question.

Q3 Change the following statements into rhetorical questions. I've done the first one for you.

- a) I think there is too much sport on television.
  Do we really need the same football match on two channels at the same time?
- b) There are too many exams for teenagers to sit.
- c) Violence is not caused by watching videos.
- d) Reading a book is often better than watching the film.
- e) Everyone should wear designer labels.
- f) It is more interesting to go abroad on holiday than to stay in this country.
- g) We should protect our environment by not dropping litter.
- h) Games consoles are changed too frequently and are too expensive.

To be or not to be — rats, I never could make decisions...

All about the structure — oh yes, it's all about the structure. *yawn* I've heard this all before. Wonder what's for tea tonight. Hope it's not beans AGAIN — I HATE beans.

Section Twelve — Writing to Persuade

Linking Arguments

Always remember — there are two sides to every argument.

Q1 Match each statement from box A with a possible counter-argument from box B. Write down both sides of the argument.

A
a) Teenagers need to play more sport.
b) Everybody should have access to the internet.
c) Every town should have a skate park.
d) People should use public transport wherever possible.
e) Mobile phones can seriously damage your health.
f) There are too many additives in food.

B
i) Public transport is not always reliable.
ii) Not everyone has a computer at home.
iii) Sports centres are expensive and not always available.
iv) Ready meals are easy and tasty.
v) Skating is not appealing to everybody.
vi) The convenience of mobile phones outweighs the dangers.

*You can use **connectives** to join opposing arguments.*

Q2 Choose some opposing arguments from Q1 and join them together using each of these connectives:

a) however
b) on the other hand
c) but
d) in contrast
e) nevertheless
f) although
g) whereas

You can also use connectives to add detail to your arguments.

Q3 Use each one of the connectives below to add detail to any of the arguments made in Q1. I've done an example for you.

a) moreover
b) in addition
c) besides
d) after all
e) therefore
f) in other words
g) meanwhile
h) furthermore
i) finally
j) not only .... but also
k) without doubt

e.g. There are too many additives in food; however, ready meals are easy and tasty. Therefore, convenience will always win over health.

Section Twelve — Writing to Persuade

Giving Advice

When you give advice it is important to make suggestions rather than give orders.

Q1 **Rewrite the following commands to make them into suggestions. I've done the first one for you.**

    a) You must choose subjects that you are good at for GCSE.
It would be best to choose subjects that you are good at for GCSE.
    b) When you want extra pocket money, make your parents a cup of tea.
It is a good idea to...
    c) Always look carefully before you cross a busy road.
    d) Make sure your homework is completed on time.
    e) Clean your teeth at least twice a day.
    f) Don't forget your best friend's birthday.
    g) Always wear clean socks when you are buying new shoes.
    h) Wear sunscreen to protect your skin.

Q2 **Choose one of the sentences from Q1 and add two more sentences which give further advice on that topic.**

Rhetorical questions can be used to give advice as well as to argue.

Q3 **Join each of the following question phrases to an ending from the box to give advice:**

    a) Why don't you...
    b) Have you thought about...
    c) Will you...
    d) What about...
    e) Could you...
    f) How about...
    g) Do you think you should...

> ...think about your option choices carefully?
> ...consider eating healthily?
> ...get some advice from your subject teacher?
> ...attending the options evening next week?
> ...asking for your parents' opinions?
> ...taking up a team sport?
> ...walk to school instead of going on the bus?

Rhetorical questions are useful for beginning a paragraph of advice.

Q4 **Choose one of the rhetorical questions above to begin a paragraph of advice on keeping yourself fit and healthy. Add at least three more suggestions similar to the ones used in Q1.**

*It's important to write with confidence and **authority**. Authority means that you know what you are talking about. Using **rhetorical questions** and words like **could** or **should** makes you sound as if you know your subject well.*

Q5 **Have a go at writing an advice leaflet for pupils in your class, on how to choose their options wisely.**

Section Twelve — Writing to Persuade

Section Thirteen — Critical Writing

Balanced Arguments

You've learnt how to persuade your readers, but you also need to know how to present a **balanced** argument.

Q1 Sort the following words into two lists. In the first list write the words that could help make your argument stronger. In the second, write the words that could change the direction of the argument and introduce a new point.

- a) whereas
- b) on the other hand
- c) therefore
- d) however
- e) as can be seen
- f) but
- g) furthermore
- h) consequently
- i) hence
- j) accordingly
- k) so
- l) conversely
- m) conflictingly
- n) in contrast
- o) in contradiction

Q2 The following ideas belong to two different sides of a situation. Write out two separate lists to show which idea belongs on which side.

- a) It is important to earn your own money.
- b) When I leave school I will learn all about banks and money.
- c) Working while at school can harm your education.
- d) Earning your own money helps you later in life to manage your money.
- e) It is good to be independent.
- f) When I have passed my exams there will be time to earn money.

Q3 Use some of the words from Q1 to help you write a paragraph giving a balanced view of working part time while still in school.

Q4 When analysing a situation it is important to use both evidence (facts) and opinion. Copy out the statements below that contain facts.

- a) 1 in 7 children surveyed own a pet
- b) I believe that it is important for all families to own a pet
- c) in 1994 the company used 3500 animals in testing
- d) statistics show that 40% of all teenagers work part-time
- e) animal testing is wrong
- f) working whilst studying harms your education
- g) being able to wear designer clothes gives you confidence
- h) of 200 teenagers surveyed, 96 of them owned a pair of Levis
- i) some people say that fast food is unhealthy

In contrast to English, Maths is very interesting...

Being able to present a balanced argument is very important, especially when it comes to writing those pesky essays. You'll need to give both sides of a situation, then draw your conclusion at the end. Learn all the connecting words in Q1 — they'll help you link your points together.

Supporting Arguments

Factual information can also be changed into opinion, to make it more persuasive.

Q1 Change the following facts into opinions. The first one has been done for you.

a) Dr Martin Luther King was assassinated in 1968 at the age of 39.
   Dr Martin Luther King was brutally murdered in his prime.
b) 3 out of every 20 boxers suffer injury in the ring.
c) 20% of all teenagers watch at least 4 hours of television a day.
d) Out of the present Year 9, 70% of them achieved a Level 5 or above.
e) The average teenager gets £5 a week pocket money.
f) 7 in 8 people surveyed prefer to eat chips rather than salad.
g) In 1990 5 out of every 10 households had a computer.
h) Do you realise that 50% of all 20 year olds have their own car.

Hint: They don't have to be facts any more. Think about what emotion you want your reader to feel.

Q2 When answering questions it may be necessary to quote from relevant passages to justify what you say. Copy out the following statements, placing quotation marks around the evidence:

a) Mark says pocket money should be £5 and I agree.
b) In the passage it states that working is essential to promote independence.
c) 'The Sun' has the largest circulation, and we're told that around 4 million copies are sold each day.
d) Slogans for products can be easily remembered; Just do it for Nike is one example.
e) The writer believes that 60% of all advertising is aimed at children.

Q3 You can also use quotations to support a point you're making. Match the following points with the correct supporting quote from the box below.

a) Macbeth was a good soldier.
b) Romeo and Juliet both came from good families.
c) Billy Casper lived in a poor house.
d) Around the world thousands of animals are used in testing.
e) Some television commercials are very short but still effective.
f) Manufactured groups do not survive for long in today's music industry.
g) Hobbits, although they live in the ground, do not have smelly, bare homes.
h) Far too many children are injured on today's roads.

i) "5 new groups fold each year"
ii) "For brave Macbeth — well he deserves that name."
iii) "10 to 20 second slots are enough to sell a product"
iv) "There were no curtains…"
v) "Two households, both alike in dignity…"
vi) "It was a hobbit-hole, and that means comfort."
vii) "12 accidents were reported last week on the City Road"
viii) "22 000 animals were tested on in France alone"

Section Thirteen — Critical Writing

Winning Arguments

Q1 Quotations don't have to be long in order to make a point. Look at the following passage and then answer the two questions that follow:

> *"For a moment the moon shone brightly enough to give a clear view of the tree bending as the wind pushed its branches to the ground."*

a) Say which words show that it was night.
b) Say which words show that it was very windy.

Read the following passage:

> *"After years of campaigning, the testing of cosmetics and toiletries on animals was finally banned in the UK on November 16th. But many animals are still being used in tests. Of the 2.6 million experiments carried out last year, only 1319 were for testing cosmetics. Some people want animal tests banned because animals feel pain and fear, just like us. Why should they suffer? Every year in Britain 3 million animals are tormented in the name of science — they are poisoned, scalded, wounded and killed."*

Q2 This writer has used facts and opinion to strengthen their argument. Copy out two facts and two opinions from the passage.

Q3 Look back to the above passage. Write down words you could quote to show that the writer is against animal testing.

Q4 Here is a list of statements about whaling. Some are for, and some are against.

> i) Between 1925 and 1975, an estimated 1.5 million whales were killed.
> ii) Without money from whaling, many coastal communities wouldn't survive.
> iii) Whales eat so much fish that they are a threat to fish stocks.
> iv) Commercial whaling during the last century wiped out most of the world's whale population.
> v) Due to the declining whale population, the International Whaling Commission agreed to the suspension of commercial whaling from 1986.
> vi) Catching whales is important for scientific research.
> vii) The whale population already faces threats from toxic pollution and climate change.
> viii) In some countries, whale meat is a traditional part of the diet.

a) Say which of the above statements you could use in an argument against whaling.

b) Should all whaling be banned? Use each of the above statements and your own opinions to give a balanced argument. Make sure you link your points together with connecting words, and then draw your own conclusion at the end.

Section Thirteen — Critical Writing

64 Section Fourteen — Writing About Drama

The Art of Performing

When you're performing there are various techniques which you can use to make your performance more interesting for the audience.

Q1 Match up the following definitions with the technique they describe from the box.

> role-play   script
> mime   improvisation

a) acting without using any sound
b) taking on the identity of a character and acting like them
c) taking on the identity of a character and acting like them without a script or practice beforehand
d) used in rehearsing a written performance

Q2 The following comments were made by students who didn't know the terms from Q1. Rewrite each comment correctly, using the above terms.

a) We worked in groups and wrote down all the words we wanted to say.
b) A group of us acted out a scene from a typical school day without using a script.
c) It was very difficult to do this performance because I kept wanting to speak.
d) After reading 'Macbeth', we put Macbeth on trial for the murder of Duncan. I pretended to be Lady Macbeth.
e) Someone else made up the play, we just performed it.
f) One of the actresses forgot her lines, so she had to make up the story as she went along.

Q3 Below is a list of tasks from a drama class. For each one, explain which of the techniques from Q1 you would use and why. (Give the answer that feels right for you.)

a) The whole class needs to be involved to discover why Macbeth killed Duncan.
b) Pick one of the ideas from the board, and act it out in small groups.
c) We never really know what happens to the characters in this play. Write a final scene showing them five years later.
d) It's important in drama to pay attention to detail. Show me how you get ready in the morning without speaking.
e) In groups of 3, pretend you're the witches plotting how to trick Macbeth.

Ground Control to Major Tom — Nicole ain't comin' back...

Being able to act like Tom Cruise is all well and good, but you've got to know a few technical terms as well. The key is to understand each technique and to know when to use it.

Section Fourteen — Writing About Drama

Reading a Play

Read through the following passage:

> A: I was going to tell you.
> B: Really?
> A: Of course I was.
>   (there's a pause)
> B: So where is it then?
> A: In the back. I put it in the back room.
> B: If it's made any kind of mess, I'm going to kill you.

Q1 How do you think the two parts should be read? Choose an answer from the following:

a) A is apologetic and B is angry.

b) A is being sarcastic and B is angry.

c) A and B are both excited.

d) A is excited and B is unimpressed.

e) It's impossible to tell without knowing where the scene comes from, or without directions to the actors.

Q2 It turns out that all the suggestions made in Q1 are wrong. Actually, A is scared and B is angry. Rewrite the passage, adding stage directions that help the actors know how to read it.

Q3 Finish off the passage quoted in Q1 to make a whole scene. Make sure there are enough stage directions to help the actors understand how to read it. (If you're stuck, look at the points below first — they'll give you a start.)

— Who are A and B?

— Where are they?

— What did A put in the back room?

— What will B find when they go in to investigate?

I laugh in the face of fear — Mwa ha ha ha ha...
And then I yell "What's that behind you" and make a dash for it in the opposite direction. Well come on — fear is all well and good, but I'd rather have a bun-cake.

Section Fourteen — Writing About Drama

Reviewing a Drama

*Drama is not just about performing. It's important that you can **write** about plays you've seen, films you've watched and television you've enjoyed.*

Q1 **Choose a film, TV drama, or play that you've seen recently, then answer the following questions about it.**

a) What was it called, and what genre (type) was it?

b) Who was in it, and what characters did they play?

c) Write down three sentences about the storyline without giving the game away.

d) What did you like / dislike about the performances?

e) Were sound effects, special lighting or music used?

f) How could it have been improved? Were the characters realistic? Was the storyline easy to follow and believable?

g) What else about the drama did you find particularly interesting?

Not your standard English teacher

Q2 **When writing a review, it's important to use the correct terms. Copy out the sentences below, inserting the missing terms from the box.**

a) When the curtains opened we could see a dining room set out for a party. The ...... showed that this was a rich family.

b) It was obvious from the ...... that the play was set in the 1900s.

c) Some parts of the stage were deliberately kept dark. This ...... was to suggest evil.

d) Without the ...... it would be difficult to realise that a train was approaching.

e) The ...... helped set the mood with fast, loud music whenever a car chase was starting.

f) By changing the ...... the director made it clear whose point of view we were seeing.

g) Whenever the characters travelled back in time the ...... were fantastic to watch.

h) The director used ...... cleverly, as Dr Evans always carried her medical bag in the back of her car.

i) The witches looked disgusting because their ...... was cleverly applied.

j) The director used ...... to make it look like the donkey was talking.

> sound track
> special effects
> make-up
> set
> lighting
> computer animation
> props
> camera angle
> sound effects
> costumes

Q3 **Using your notes from Q1 and the list of key terms from Q2, write a short review of a film, a TV drama or a performance that you've seen.**

Section Fourteen — Writing About Drama

The Answers

Section 1 — Spelling

Page 1

Q1 a) deserts
    b) country
    c) estuary
    d) pollution
    e) whether, weather

Q2 Bob Angelo has been painting and drawing **sketches** for years. He is most famous for his **collage** showing Burger King in the **foreground** of Venice. In particular, his use of **acrylic** paints **highlights** his incredible skill with a **palette**. His work is currently on **exhibition** at the Tate Modern.

Q3 a) equilateral, isosceles, scalene
    b) reflectional, symmetry
    c) parallelogram, rhombus, quadrilaterals
    d) measured, metres, tonnes
    e) horizontal, perpendicular, vertical

Q4 a) The brothers always <u>contradict</u> each other.
    b) The Houses of <u>Parliament</u> are in London.
    c) King Mordred laid <u>siege</u> to Paris.
    d) It can be difficult to move to Australia because of the <u>immigration</u> laws.
    e) An alien <u>civilisation</u> could be very advanced.
    f) The story is told in <u>chronological</u> order.

Page 2

Q1 They all sound very similar.

Q2 any reasonable answers — for example:
    b) r<u>i</u>de, h<u>i</u>gh, p<u>i</u>e, goodb<u>y</u>e, sk<u>y</u>
    c) w<u>or</u>d, l<u>ear</u>n, s<u>er</u>ve, c<u>ur</u>se, j<u>our</u>ney,
    d) p<u>ier</u>, d<u>ear</u>, b<u>eer</u>, adh<u>ere</u>
    e) sp<u>are</u>, b<u>ear</u>, th<u>ere</u>, th<u>eir</u>, p<u>air</u>

Q3 a) say, soy
    b) staid, steed, stood, stead
    c) although
    d) bitter, better, batter, butter
    e) lovely, lively
    f) lonely
    g) light
    h) height
    i) weight
    j) wait
    k) relief
    l) receive
    m) weird
    n) beautiful
    o) woman, women
    p) given
    q) jolly, jelly
    r) jealous

Q4 The words that don't follow the rule are *height*, *weight* and *weird*.

Page 3

Q1 a) tagged, tagging
    b) dropped, dropping
    c) shopped, shopping
    d) hummed, humming
    e) prodded, prodding
    f) stepped, stepping
    g) netted, netting
    h) jogged, jogging

Q2 a) lazy, lazier, laziest
    b) flashy, flashier, flashiest
    c) multiply, multiplies, multiplied
    d) qualify, qualifies, qualified

Q3 a) stories
    b) foxes
    c) kites
    d) quantities
    e) buses
    f) marches
    g) kisses
    h) frequencies
    i) spies
    j) wishes
    k) larboratories
    l) lice

Page 4

Q1 b) unnecessary
    c) immoral
    d) misunderstood
    e) dissatisfied
    f) illegal
    g) indiscreet
    h) irregular

Q2 a) formidable
    b) collapsible
    c) invincible
    d) undrinkable
    e) inevitable

Q3 a) cemetery
    b) stationary
    c) stationery
    d) dictionary
    e) confectionery

Q4 a) difference
    b) conference
    c) acceptance
    d) brilliance
    e) relevance

Q5 a) Egyptian
    b) collision
    c) discussion
    d) optician
    e) emotion

Page 5

Q1 any reasonable answers

Q2 any reasonable answers

Q3 any reasonable answers

Q4 1 magician, electrician, physician, optician, musician
    2 physicist, dentist, physiotherapist
    3 telescope, kaleidoscope, microscope, periscope
    4 happier, easier, angrier, friendlier
    5 biology, sociology, psychology, cosmology
    6 capricious, outrageous, ferocious, delicious, malicious

Page 6

Q1 all begin with the same set of letters, suggesting a common root, and hence related meanings:
    a) 'necess-', needful
    b) 'vis-', having to do with seeing / sight.
    c) 'argu-', to quarrel
    d) 'differ-', unlike
    e) 'know-', be aware of, have in your mind.
    f) 'resist-', stop

Q2 a) keep
    b) drop
    c) keep

Q3 any reasonable answers— for example:
    a) knight, knife, knee, knew, knowledge
    b) write, who, wrap, wrong, whole
    c) though, thought, daughter, night, weigh
    d) stripe, tale, fare, trade, bone
    e) honest, rhino, hour, rhyme, rhythm
    f) climb, debt, subtle, lamb, comb
    g) psalm, pneumonia, pterodactyl, psychology, pseudonym

Q4 a) axes
    b) media
    c) formulae
    d) hippopotami

Page 7

Q1 There are six mistakes in the sentence, but the spellchecker would only pick up one of them.

Q2 a) biscuit
    b) knife
    c) rhubarb
    d) receive
    e) churches
    f) shield
    g) potatoes
    h) puppies
    i) leaves
    j) welcome
    k) travelling
    l) loving
    m) manageable
    n) cried

The Answers

The Answers

Q3 a) amphibian
    b) mammal
    c) vertebrate
    d) triceps
    e) composition
    f) kilometres
    g) foreign

Section 2 — Vocabulary

Page 8

Q1 b) main clause
    c) adverb
    d) noun
    e) adjective
    f) passive verb
    g) subordinate clause

Q2 (there are other possibilities)
    <u>noun</u>: trip / picnic / provisions / boatyard / night / boat / work
    <u>adjective</u>: gorgeous
    <u>verb</u>: went / was / took off / pack / knew / make / were / spend / had
    <u>passive verb</u>: was had
    <u>main clause</u>: The children would have liked to spend the night on the boat
    <u>subordinate clause</u>: but unfortunately both David and I had to go to work today.
    <u>adverb</u>: absolutely / unfortunately

Q3 a) She's obviously not as clever as you. — comparison
    b) Peter pointedly placed a piece of pepperoni on his plate. — alliteration
    c) He's as white as a sheet. — simile
    d) He squelched through the mud. — onomatopoeia
    e) How can I compete with this giant? — metaphor
    f) I thought I saw the tall one yawn this morning. — assonance

Page 9

Q1 a) Jane was not the easiest person in the world to live with. — difficult to get on with
    b) Elizabeth has firm principles. — stubborn
    c) Jack always has a great deal to say for himself. — talks too much
    d) Custard isn't her favourite food. — really doesn't like it
    e) He has limited experience in this field. — knows hardly anything about it
    f) The government is considering the differing views which have been expressed. — hasn't decided what to do
    g) It's well known that the two men do not have an easy relationship. — can't stand each other

Q2 Possible answers:
    a) Get your books out.
    b) Start at the beginning.
    c) Don't do that.

Q3 Possible answers:
    a) a bias in information to give a favourable impression
       also means twist/turn around; a twisting/circular movement
    b) consequence; result(s)
       also means radiation from a nuclear bomb
    c) route; way; means; way of achieving
       also means street
    d) section; department
       also means table for writing on

Q4 a) i) They were wringing their hands nervously.
       It's no use MPs wringing their hands now.
       ii) We decided to meet them halfway, at the pub.
       We're going to have to meet them halfway on this.
       iii) They were sitting on the sofa.
       They've been sitting on these documents for months.
       iv) I'm just finishing the icing on the cake.
       Her new job's the icing on the cake.
       v) The first runner was handing over the baton when he slipped.
       He won't be handing over the baton just yet.
       vi) Wispy clouds were hanging in the air.
       She left her remark hanging in the air, and disappeared.

    possible answers:
    b) i) It's no use MPs acting as if they're sorry now.
       ii) We're going to have to compromise on this.
       iii) They've had these documents for months, and failed to deal with them.
       iv) Her new job's the latest or best in a series of good things that have happened.
       v) He won't be handing over responsibility to another person just yet.
       vi) She didn't wait for a reply before disappearing.

Page 10

Q1 a) in spite of this / nevertheless / although / despite this / however
    b) in addition to this… / moreover / furthermore
    c) because of this… / as a result of this… / a consequence of this was… / consequently
    d) following the… / subsequently / later

Q2 a) You look upstairs while I check if he's outside.
    b) In order to allow us to check our records, please fill in your details below.
    c) In general it seems quite good, although I can't comment on the details.
    d) I won't be able to help you unless you tell me what the problem is.
    e) We need to know your name so that we can tick you off on the register.
    f) Since he hasn't arrived, we'll start without him.
    g) Jane was still finishing the first exercise. Meanwhile, Jack had started the next one.

Q3 any reasonable answers

Section 3 — Sentences and Paragraphs

Page 11

Q1 a) I asked her to phone me as soon as she arrived.
    b) Please let us know if we can be of any further assistance.
    c) How would you like it if it happened to you?
    d) These are the things you'll need: pyjamas, underwear, sleeping bag, soap, toothpaste, toothbrush and comb.
    e) I don't know why he came — he knew we were okay.
    f) Having seen the photos, I wish I'd been there.

Q2 Suggested answers:
    a) The unfortunate animal was eventually found in its hiding place, which was halfway up a tree at the bottom of the garden. It was brought back down after a neighbour lent an extra long ladder. The ladder was only just long enough to reach the cat, which by now was absolutely terrified.

    b) I phoned the station yesterday to ask about train times. Actually, I phoned twice, because you often get told different things. Then I rang Lucy, who told me she'd been told something completely different. In fact, what she'd been told was different from the two pieces of information I'd received.

    c) There weren't enough parents to help with transport, so we couldn't go on the trip. It was a shame really, as the whole class (apart from Jack) was looking forward to it, even though we'd heard some pretty scary stories about white-water rafting. In fact, I'm not sure why Jack was scared; he's usually one of the most adventurous in the

The Answers

The Answers

class and will generally have a go at anything.

Q3 everything is true except d).

Page 12

Q1 comma , between some clauses / between items in a list / before direct speech
full stop . between sentences
question mark ? after a question
exclamation mark ! after a sentence which is very emphatic
semicolon ; between sentences which you want to join together and between items in a list where some of the items are multiple words containing commas
colon : to introduce something, for example a list

Q2 a) Don't worry if you can't come — we'll send you what you need.
b) I'll get your coat — don't forget to pick up your bags.
c) Metals are good conductors; non-metals are good insulators.
d) There will be several room changes this week; please consult the lists on the noticeboards.
e) Don't download your e-mail — your virus protection isn't up to date.

Q3 a) My mother, who's seventy-six, can remember the war.
b) I'd like to see Jane, Phil and Peter after assembly.
c) Could anyone who has seen my camera please tell me?
d) If you ask, I'm sure he'll help you.
e) Could you remind me to water the plants before we go?
f) However we do this, it won't be easy.
g) He's convinced it's the right thing to do. However, I'm not.

Q4 a) You can use a colon before a list. You'll need the following: a packed lunch, drinks, spare clothes and a sunhat.
b) You can use a colon before a quotation, especially a long one. To paraphrase a friend of mine: some people live a long time before realising that they're actually very happy.
c) A colon is sometimes used to show that an explanation, or more information, is about to be given. He told me there was no need to worry: he had examined her and decided that a trip to hospital was not necessary.

Page 13

Q1 [some of these are suggestions only, as other answers are possible for some words]
b) was not / wasn't
c) notwithstanding / despite
d) moreover / what's more
e) facilitate / make possible
f) reprimand / tell off
g) ensure / make sure
h) aggressive / in-your-face
i) nevertheless / but, however
j) excellent / wicked

Q2 a) The matter was discussed at length.
We had a really long talk about the whole thing.
b) The full effects of using this medicine have not yet been properly investigated.
No one's tried to find out the effects of this medicine yet.
c) A new peace deal has been brokered.
They've sorted out a new peace deal.
d) More goods are imported than are exported.
They import more than they export.
e) Germany was reunified in 1990.
They joined Germany together again in 1990.
f) A decision was finally reached, but not before several points of view had been aired.
We finally reached a decision, but only after hearing lots of opinions.

Q3 a) Further work remains to be done.
b) The growth of new industries continued throughout this period.
c) Consultation with the public will, of course, continue.

Page 14

Q1 a) "I really adored chocolate when I was young," said Deirdre.
b) Deirdre declared her childhood love of chocolate.
c) "Neither of us did it," said the boys.
d) Both parties maintained their innocence.
e) "You know I'll love you forever," she murmured.
f) She told him she would always love him.

Q2 **Exact words**
He called him a "shining example".
Members have called for "a fresh approach".
Not necessarily exact words
He said she was lazy and uncooperative.
They threatened to call a referendum.
She says he's working too hard.

Q3 As I walked along the High Street, I noticed a sign in the village shop saying "Puppies for Sale". I pushed open the door and went in. The woman behind the counter told me there were four puppies who were three weeks old. She said the father was a labrador and the mother was a retriever.
"Can I see them?" I asked.
"Of course," she replied, and led me through a door at the back of the shop.

Q4 a) In the final chapter, the hero is described as "a man without hope".
b) He referred to him as "a callous and insensitive coward".
c) She said later that he should "mind his own business".
d) They used to call me "Forgetful Flo" because of my terrible memory.

Page 15

Q1 a) Dogs, on the other hand, are a completely different story.
b) Dogs
c) on the other hand; a completely different story

Q2 Paragraph/Begins/Talks about
1st / Most families argue… / basic problem - arguing over TV - + solutions
2nd / If you have satellite… / further problem - satellite TV
3rd / An alternative to arguing… / alternative solution - don't watch TV
4th / To be even more radical… / more radical solution - don't have TV

Page 16

Q1 a) When choosing a new floor covering, consider the following points.
b) Do you need something that is easily cleaned (a hard floor), or something that is warm and comfortable (a soft carpet)? Don't forget that a hard floor is much noisier and colder than a carpet. Of course, you can have the best of both worlds by using rugs on top of a hard surface.
c) consider; following points

Q2 [answers may vary]
1st paragraph refers back to earlier in the day.
2nd paragraph refers back to Peter's phone call.
3rd paragraph refers back to the writer's advice on telling lies.
4th paragraph refers back to the question of whether Peter would come or not.

Q3 everything except e)

Q4 a) There are several ways to get in touch with us. You can phone us, send us a text or e-mail, fax us, or even put a letter in the post.
b) As he walked along the street he had a sudden sense of having been there before. But he did not recognise the stone buildings or cobbled road surfaces.
c) Later that day he received a text message from his girlfriend. She

The Answers

wanted some help with her homework.

Section 4 — Different Types of Non-Fiction

Page 17

Q1 a) The Shetland Islands are a group of islands <u>just up from, and a bit right of,</u> the Orkneys. In the 9th century, <u>those Norse types sneaked in</u> and <u>took over</u> the islands. Then in 1472, Scotland <u>nicked</u> them. The people <u>do loads of fishing</u>, and the islands are famous for <u>those cute</u> <u>little</u> Shetland Ponies.

b) any reasonable answer
Here's an example:
The Shetland Islands are a group of islands north-east of the Orkneys. In the 9th century the islands were settled by Norse invaders. In 1472, they were seized by Scotland. Fishing is important to the islanders, and the islands are famous for Shetland Ponies.

Q2 a) formal
b) informal
c) formal

Q3 any reasonable answer

Page 18

Q1 to Q4: any reasonable answers

Page 19

Q1 any reasonable answers— for example: the Internet, mobile phones, pagers, satellite TV / phones, CD-ROMS etc.

Q2 any reasonable answers— for example:
a) a book is easy to access but may not have up to date information.
b) you can only use a CD-ROM if you have a computer, but they're interactive

Q3, Q4: any reasonable answers

Q5 any reasonable answer — for example:

Hi Uncle Dave

I know you're a Man Utd fan, so I was wondering if you'd like to come round and watch the football tonight. It should be a great game — I'm really looking forward to an exciting battle between the old enemies! Lots of my friends are coming round, so it should be a fun evening.

Hope to see you later
Phil

Section 5 — Varieties of English

Page 20

Q1 a) I did better than I expected to.
b) They were waiting for someone to help them.
c) I was right.
d) She was still hungry.
e) It doesn't have to be like this.
f) I saw him yesterday.
g) Jane did it.
h) I have never seen it. / I've never seen it. / I haven't ever seen it.
i) She gave it to me.
j) I'll do it afterwards.
k) The man who / that came yesterday was a bit strange.

Q2 a) He said it wasn't very good.
b) She finished them very quickly.
c) He said he would come (round) to our house at about 5 o'clock.
d) John's new car (or bike) is very nice.
e) No, I was looking at the other one.
f) Could you throw me a packet of crisps? Thank you.

Q3 a) He was constantly changing his mind.
b) He may agree.
c) It seemed incredible to everyone.
d) A great effort was made to resolve the situation.

Page 21

Q1 **Thank you** for your letter.
I am sorry to hear that you **did not** enjoy your meal.
Perhaps you would have enjoyed something from our à la carte menu.
Please find enclosed a voucher which will entitle you to a **complimentary** meal at any of our restaurants.

Q2 any reasonable answer — for example:
When we **were** children people **were not** allowed to waste anything. We made everything **go a long way** — almost everything **was** rationed, and our **mother** would **punish** us for throwing away anything **which was still useful**.

Food **was** still rationed and you had to be very inventive. We ate everything **that was** put in front of us. No one ever said they didn't like **anything**.

In **those** days we didn't have **any** modern vacuum cleaners and washing machines. They **were** too expensive for **ordinary people like us**. We had to work **much** harder to do the housework but you never heard **anyone** complaining. In those days we knew how to clean things **properly**. We weren't lazy like you young **people**.

Q3 a) Conversation. **We will** see what **we are** doing later.
b) Conversation. **I asked**, "Why can't we go in through here?" and **he said**, "Use the other entrance madam," **in a rather self-important manner**.
c) E-mail or informal letter. **While we were on holiday in France I** went white-water rafting. It was **excellent**. I got knocked about in the boat. It was scary and exciting. **I won't ever** forget it, especially while **I** still have **the** bruises!
d) Text message. Your present was great. Thank you.
e) Conversation. That's the one I lent to Joshua. Why is he giving it to you?
f) Informal written note or phone / voice message. Jen, I shall be out until around four o'clock. Tell Steve to phone me and tell me at what time he wants to be picked up. If you go to the shops, don't spend all of your allowance. I shall see you later, Mum.
g) E-mail, conversation or Internet message board. Please don't take everything so seriously.

Page 22

Q1 They're all true.

Q2 a) bun; bap; <u>cob</u>
b) <u>snicket</u>; footpath; <u>ginnel</u>; alley; alleyway; passage
c) <u>mom</u>; <u>mam</u>; ma; mummy; <u>mommy</u>; mother; <u>mama</u>; <u>mater</u>; old woman
d) daddy; <u>pa</u>; <u>papa</u>; father; old man; <u>pater</u>; pop
e) frozen; bitterly cold; <u>starved</u>; perishing; chilled to the bone
f) moody; bad-tempered; <u>mardy</u>; grouchy

Q3 any sensible answers — will depend on dialects you're familiar with.

Q4 any sensible answers — will depend on dialects you're familiar with.

Q5 a) There are too many of us to go in one car.
b) I did / have done really well.
c) Not one of these issues is important.
d) She asked if she could borrow his pen.
e) There are several new books.

Page 23

Q1 any reasonable answers— for example:
a) My take on the situation is different.
b) They're trying to level the playing field by ensuring that everyone has the same opportunities.
c) You can text me.
d) Can you scan this photo for me?
e) I run virus-checking software every

The Answers

day.

Q2 any reasonable answers— for example:
a) I got it from the hardware store. / Is it a hardware or software problem?
b) Can you put it on disc? / They were sticking little discs of paper onto their pictures.
c) I've got a terrible memory. / How much memory does your computer have?
d) Do you know how to juggle? / She was trying to juggle work and looking after the family.
e) Help me wrap up Pete's present. / Shall we wrap things up now?
f) Put it down on the ground. / Personnel on the ground report continued disturbances.

Q3 a) makeover — DIY show
b) mulching — gardening show
c) pro-vitamin — advertisement
d) shooter — American crime thriller
e) barbie — Australian soap

Q4 a) **eco**-warrior — new prefix
b) **nimby** — new acronym
c) **Do you want to phone a friend?** — new catchphrase
d) "You know Jane?" "Yeah - she's **well** clever." — new use of word within sentence
e) **screensaver** — new compound noun
f) **move the goalposts** — new phrase

Q5 note — other meanings are also possible in some cases.
A: no longer used
whither = to where
liege = lord
behold = look

B: has a different old meaning
fond = foolish
nice = precise
charity = love/concern
wilt = will
gentle = noble/chivalrous
ozone = fresh air

Section 6 — Research and Study Skills

Page 24

Q1 a) library
b) Internet
c) encyclopedia
d) television
e) other people
f) newspaper

Q2 any reasonable answer

Q3 a) loquat
b) blaff
c) dasheen / taro and Chinese spinach

Page 25

Q1 A formal written English
B informal spoken English
C informal written English
D informal spoken English

Q2 B trying to persuade to wear harnesses
C illustrating how harnesses can save lives
D doesn't want to wear a harness

Q3 any reasonable answer

Page 26

Q1 any reasonable answer — for example:
Yes, because the uniform is far too hot for summer.
No, if she didn't look smart.

Q2 any reasonable answer

Q3 quite personal

Q4 any reasonable answer — for example:
interview the other staff
review the uniform policy
ask customers

Q5 any reasonable answer

Page 27

Q1 any reasonable answers

Q2 any reasonable answers— for example:
a) copying out key words / topic sentences
drawing flowcharts
drawing diagrams
using IT to change the text into your own version
b) writing in the margin of your own books
underlining
keywords / topic sentences
recording your spoken notes and ideas onto tape
c) writing in the margin of your own books
underlining
highlighting in different colours
writing comments on sticky notes
keywords / topic sentences
drawing a flowchart
drawing a mindmap or spider diagram

Q3 any reasonable answers

Page 28

Q1 a) unreliable
b) irrelevant
c) trustworthy
d) irrelevant
e) unreliable
f) trustworthy

Q2 3m x 3m pool
minigolf only open Tuesday 7-9pm
2500 rooms
self-catering

Q3 any reasonable answer

Page 29

Q1 Ever since the poetry of Chaucer, rhyme has been closely **associated** with **rhythm** in English poetry**.** It is also to be found in the early poems and songs of many **languages**. For most English speakers, the first time they meet it is in the form of **nursery** rhymes, many of which involve numbers (e.g. "One, two, / Buckle my shoe"). This fact supports the theory that rhyme may have **originated** (**no comma**) in primitive religious rites and magic spells. From such early beginnings, poetry has **had** strong links with music — the **earliest** ballads were designed to be sung — and rhyme has been a crucial element in the musicality of poetry. **It** has also been responsible, in large part, for making poetry **memorable**.
It often has a more subtle function as well, one **which** may not be **immediately** apparent. By linking one rhyming word with another, poets may introduce associations which confirm, question, or on occasion deny the literal meaning of their words.
Although the most common rhymes consist of only one or two **syllables** (e.g. lay / way, dreaming / **scheming**), triple and even quadruple **rhymes** are to be found — often in comic verse. A particularly good example is W. S. Gilbert's "I Am the Very Model of a Modern Major-General**"**, with lines such as:
"I'm very well **aquainted** too with matters mathe*matical*,
I understand equations, both the simple and qua*dratical*."

Q2 all of them except f)

Page 30

Q1 d)

Q2 a) trustworthy
b) untrustworthy
c) objective
d) subjective
e) viewpoint
f) authorial voice
g) biased

Q3 any reasonable answers— for example:
a) feels stifled by the rest of the community.
b) is comforted by a close community.

The Answers

Q4 a) biased
    b) reliable
    c) biased

Page 31

Q1 any reasonable answers — these are examples of points that could be made:
    A advertisement:
       big, bold statement of offer
       picture
       small print
       very little text
    B recipe:
       name of recipe emphasised
       number it serves
       clear list of ingredients
    C music review:
       name of band and name of album emphasised
       music jargon e.g. "'70s wah-wah funk"
       author's name at the foot of the text
    D poem:
       title and author emphasised
       line-breaks important
       capital letter at the beginning of each line
       rhythm
    E newspaper article:
       large headline
       two columns

Page 32

Q1 any reasonable answer

Q2 any reasonable answer

Q3 b)

Q4 a), b), c) or d) — the answer is purely subjective

Q5 no

Section 7 — Author's Craft

Page 33

Q1 a) 1 b) 2 c) 1 d) 2 e) 2 f) 1

Q2 anxiety, love, secrecy, loss, regret

Q3 a) 1st person narrative — both poems use "I"
    b) form — both poems are written as three quatrains (four-line verses)
    c) metre — Never Seek has four regular beats on most lines, while The Secret alternates four beats with three.

Q4 1. b), c), d), e), g)
    2. a), f)

Page 34

Q1 any reasonable answers

Q2 a) ii) b) iii) c) i)

Q3 True — b), c), d), e), f), g)
    (some of these may be open to discussion)

Page 35

Q1 any reasonable answers— for example:
    a) People are fed up with the gangs terrorising their area.
    b) There isn't enough to do on the estate, which is why there is trouble.
    c) The trouble is small scale, but keeps recurring.

Q2 possible answers:
    a) same side — b)
       against — a) and c) (or just a))
    b) extract a) — Headline; "notorious" tells the reader the estate already has a bad reputation; "reeling" suggests being knocked off balance with shock; "gangs" is used in plural even though there was just one…etc.
       extract c) — the final sentence shows that this is not the first time this sort of thing has happened, etc.
    c) in extract a) they say there were 30 boys but in extract c) that there were 12. The bigger number makes the group's action sound more threatening and dramatic. Also in a) it says the boys were 'setting fire to bins', whereas c) mentions a single bin emitting smoke. Again a) is made to sound more dramatic.
    d) a) — probably a local paper sensationalising the story to increase reader interest.
       b) — Housing Officer is campaigning for more to be done by the council in his / her area of responsibility.
       c) — police report records facts to refer to later in court if needed and the language weighs slightly against the boys because the police want to do what they can to ensure that the boys stop behaving like that.

Q3 a) i) Don't challenge the government because they have access to all the information on the subject.
       ii) Why is there no satisfactory answer coming from the government?
    b) i) Kerry is independent and self-confident.
       ii) Kerry looks strange / different from everyone else.
    c) i) Animal suffering must stop.
       ii) There is no such thing as suffering in animals.

Page 36

Q1 a) how can you allow / poor, suffering little / any longer
    b) seems to think
    c) what is..? / struggle, struggle and still more struggle
    d) interesting (four times)
    e) we are / we don't / million years

Q2 i) used in e)
    ii) used in e)
    iii) used in a) and c)
    iv) used in e)
    v) used in a)
    vi) used in b)
    vii) used in c) and d)
    viii) used in a)
    ix) used in a)

Q3 a) no b) yes c) yes d) no

Q4 any reasonable answers— for example:
    b) Well you can think of me lying on a beach soaking up the sunshine, while you're sitting inside watching the rain.
    c) If you don't go now, you might never get the chance again.
    d) Don't worry grandad, at least if the plane crashes you won't get eaten by those nasty crocodiles!

Section 8 — Literary Texts

Page 37

Q1 any answer along the lines of 'pretty and picturesque'

Q2 spring

Q3 any reasonable answer

Q4, Q5: any reasonable answers

Q6 a) to destroy his 'evil eye'
    b) no

Q7 any reasonable answer

Page 38

Q1 The exclamations (shown by exclamation marks) suggest that Lady Macbeth is very excited and also, perhaps, indicate that the actress should either call them out in a loud voice or have an urgent tone. She is excited because Macbeth's letter has made her ambitious for him and she wants to share with him her ideas for making him King of Scotland.

Q2 What you wrote in your letter has set my imagination going, and I feel that we are already in the future and you are King.

Q3 This use of imperative or command verbs

The Answers

shows that Lady Macbeth is taking charge of the situation and that her husband should follow her instructions. This would have been unusual at a time when women were meant to obey their husbands, not vice versa. It also prepares us for the fact that Macbeth does, in fact, follow his wife's murder plan against his own better judgement. She also wants her husband to leave all the planning and preparation for the murder to her.

Q4 She is instructing him to deceive the King, who they intend to murder, by appearing to be pleasant (like a flower) but in actual fact to be evil and ready to kill (like a serpent). Remember that in the Bible the devil sometimes takes the form of a venomous snake.

Q5 Macbeth is firstly trying to show to his wife that he is still in charge. This is why he says that he wants to talk to her again about the murder plot. He is also trying to hint to her that she is jumping the gun by discussing how to kill the King when they have not yet talked about whether they should do such a thing. Macbeth is continually troubled about whether it is morally right to kill to achieve your ambitions.

Q6 Lady Macbeth has been given almost nine times as many words as Macbeth. This means that she is often the person who the audience pay most attention to and this again implies that she is the more powerful of the two. Notice how all the planning is done by Lady Macbeth, while her husband can only respond or try to delay her.

Q7 Lady Macbeth chooses to use her husband's titles, one of which is very recent. Shakespeare does this to suggest that she is more concerned with her husband's career than with their relationship as man and wife. In contrast, Macbeth appears to relate to Lady Macbeth principally as a loving husband. This again demonstrates that Lady Macbeth is mainly excited about meeting her husband because she can now plot his career, while Macbeth is simply pleased to see her because she is his wife.

Page 39

Q1 any reasonable answers— for example:
   a) A young woman was expected to marry someone who would increase the social standing or wealth of her family. For someone to marry outside their own class was seriously frowned upon.
   b) It was the woman's place to marry well, for the good of her family.

Q2 any reasonable answers— for example:
   a) Men were very tired and ill-equipped: "Men marched asleep. Many had lost their boots"
   b) The general tone of the poem is one of disgust at the conditions the men suffered. When he writes in the first person, he describes the terror of his dreams — reliving the nightmare visions of the trenches.
   c) Suggests that war was seen as a glorious and noble thing in society at the time.
   d) Owen wrote about a very important part of the World's history from a very human point of view. He wrote about the nature of the human spirit, and the horrific realities of war. Since the world seems bent on making war a recurring theme, Wilfred Owen's work is just as relevant today as it was over 80 years ago.

Page 40

Q1 any reasonable answer — for example: "After supper, she took out her book and taught me about someone called Moses and the Bulrushes. I was really eager to find out all about him, but she eventually revealed that Moses had been dead for a very long time. So then I no longer really cared about him because I am not interested in dead people."

Q2 any reasonable answers, which could include these points:
   i) The author uses 'and' as the main connective in the sentences. This is done to convey the impression that Huck is speaking directly to the reader and that he has quite simple language. The other main connective (linking word) is 'but' and this is because Huckleberry Finn has a lot of problems dealing with living with the widow.
   ii) The author uses repetition to show how uncomfortable Huck is, for example, his new clothes make him "sweat" and so does his eagerness to find out about Moses. However, the repetition of 'but' shows his disappointment with his new life.
   iii) A dialect word Twain uses for food is "victuals". An example of an American vernacular phrase (this means the way Americans speak) is: "I don't take no stock in ..." which means "I am not interested in..."
   iv) The author also conveys a lot about Huck's character by allowing him to talk about himself and so revealing his attitudes towards the widow.

Page 41

Q1 any reasonable answer — for example: 'Windy Nights': the poet begins by setting the scene. He says that whenever it is a stormy night with the clouds hiding the moon and the stars and it is raining heavily, then a nameless rider can be heard to gallop by. The poet wonders why the rider is out on such wild nights. The second verse repeats this idea though now he emphasises the wind thrashing at the trees on land and the ships on the sea. Again he tells the reader that the rider chooses such nights to ride down the highway and then later return.

'Meeting at Night': again the poet begins by setting the scene. It is night and the poet paints an image of a sea shore lit by a half moon so that the waves appear to be on fire with this light. The narrator describes how he lands his boat in a bay before setting off across fields to a farm where he knocks on a window and lights a match as a signal to the woman he loves. The conclusion is very romantic.

Q2 any reasonable answers— for example:
similarities
both take place at night
both give the reader a picture
both are mysterious
both are written in two verses
differences
stormy night compared with calm
Windy Nights has no real ending but Meeting does
Meeting has a first person narrator
Meeting is a kind of love poem whereas Windy Nights is more scary
Meeting tells more of a story

Q3 any reasonable answers

Q4 any reasonable answers

Q5 Examples of repetition: 'Windy Night': "by","whenever", "gallop"; 'Meeting at Night': "and", "each".

Q6 any reasonable answers— for example:
'Windy Nights'
Is he a ghost? Where does he go? Why does he only gallop on stormy nights? Is he a highwayman or robber?
'Meeting at Night'
Who is the narrator? Is the narrator the man or the woman in the relationship? Why do they meet in secret? Are they running away to get married?

Q7 any reasonable answer

Page 42

Q1 a) They all imply physical discomfort — his feet hurt (limping) and he is freezing cold — hugging and clasping himself.
   b) Simile 'like a man whose legs were numbed and stiff' suggests that he is cold and that this has made his whole body rigid; looks as if dead people are pursuing him — this suggests that death is trying to catch him; in the last paragraph about the pirate it almost implies he is trying to

The Answers

kill himself.

c) Effect of repetition of black adds to dreary atmosphere and also colour is associated with death and fear.

Q2 any reasonable answers, e.g.
When the convict asks for a promise, he says: 'Say Lord strike you dead if you don't' — a very childish oath.
The narrator is described as having 'young eyes'.

Q3 any reasonable answer

Q4 any reasonable answer

Q5 any reasonable answer

Section 9 — Essay Skills

Page 43

Q1 a) journal / diary
b) instruction manual
c) poem
d) newspaper report
e) letter
f) legal document

Q2 a) letter
b) newspaper article or journal
c) instructions

Q3 any reasonable answers

Page 44

Q1 any reasonable answer— for example:
A duck disappeared. People thought a fox ate it, but in fact it was a chicken with a grudge.

Q2 any reasonable answer — for example:
There are ducks at the golf course.
One duck disappeared last week.
A fox had been seen in the area prior to the disappearance.
A series of large scratches was found in the ground at the scene of the crime.
There is reputed to be a rivalry between chickens and ducks in the area.
A chicken was found carrying a fox costume.
The costume-carrying culprit escaped.

Q3 c)
not a) because it wasn't a fox
not b) because it wasn't a chicken that was taken
not d) because the chicken didn't have a gun

Q4 any reasonable answer

Page 45

Q1 a), b) and c) apply to the passage

Q2 formal — a), d), e)
informal — b), c), f)

Q3 any reasonable answer

Q4 any reasonable answer

Page 46

Q1 and Q2: any reasonable answers

Section 10 — Writing Fiction

Page 47

Q1 a) war
b) mystery
c) science fiction
d) action
e) romance
f) animal stories
g) horror

Q2 any reasonable answers

Q3 any reasonable answers— for example:

b) Fear written all over their faces, the soldiers cowered in the damp trenches.
c) The spaceship, spinning out of control, hurtled towards the burning planet.
d) The young man nervously approached the beautiful model.
e) Convinced she heard footsteps, she glanced behind her into the shadows.
f) Terrence, tired after his adventures, retreated into his shell.
g) The snow charged down the mountain side, roaring like an express train, towards the stricken climbers.

Page 48

Q1 c), e), a), d), f), b)

Q2 b), f), c), a), d), e).

Q3 a) Life returned to normal, until the next time.
b) The alarm clock sounded. It was the 7th of September, all over again!
c) At last they had found the serial killer, but had they found all the victims?
d) They were together again at last, but for how long?
e) Not a hair flickered on the slaughtered bodies as they lay scattered on the bloody field.
f) The boat, silhouetted against the sunset, carried the two lovers to their destiny.
g) "You will never defeat me!" cackled the vampire.

Q4 any reasonable answers

Page 49

Q1 A <u>glorious</u> day had begun. The <u>powder-blue</u> sky was dotted with <u>cotton-wool</u> clouds. A swallow flitted through the <u>still</u> air, her <u>sharp</u> wings slicing a path effortlessly. Her turns were <u>swift</u> and <u>precise</u>; she was <u>supreme</u>. Below her on the <u>tiny country</u> lanes, <u>red-faced</u> humans crawled along in their <u>metal</u> coffins, sweating and sighing their way to the <u>crowded</u> beaches.

Q2 any reasonable answer

Q3 a) huge
b) minute
c) ancient
d) new-born
e) recent
f) useful
g) pleasant
h) awful

Q4 any reasonable answers

Q5 a) bull b) snail c) fox d) dog
e) mule f) cat g) ox h) fish

Page 50

Q1 any reasonable answers

Q2 a) pun b) alliteration c) commands
d) rhetorical question e) adjectives

Q3 any reasonable answers

Q4 a) A RIGHT PAIR OF KNICKERS
b) FIRE BREAKS OUT AT BECKINGHAM PALACE
c) GROUNDS FOR OPTIMISM?
d) TOO COLD TO BARE ALL ON BEACHES
e) BATON BECKONS FOR BARBARA
f) THE PLAICE TO EAT!

Page 51

Q1 a) Wrapped up in a five-pound note.
b) Glorious, the sun.
c) And found that he only had two.
d) In the forests of the night,
e) Where civil blood makes civil hands unclean

Q2 a) limerick = c)
b) sonnet = e)
c) haiku = b)
d) regular rhyming scheme = a)
e) rhyming couplets = d)

Q3 any reasonable answers

The Answers

Section 11 — Writing Information

Page 52

Q1 a), c), and d) give information clearly

Q2 answers may vary slightly:
    b) Romeo and Juliet was written a long time ago so the language can seem strange.
    e) Running a marathon takes time and is very tiring.
    f) The England football team play in white at home and in red away.
    g) The London Eye goes very high and gives excellent views across London.

Q3 a) musician
    b) acid rain
    c) Commonwealth
    d) Big Brother
    e) regular exercise
    f) astronaut

Q4 Neil Armstrong = a), c) & e)
    acid rain = b), d) & f)

Q5 any reasonable answer

Page 53

Q1 a) should
    b) could
    c) must
    d) must
    e) could

Q2 a) might not
    b) must not
    c) won't
    d) should not

Q3 any reasonable answers

Page 54

Q1 a) It is important to drive slowly past schools **because** children may be playing nearby.
    b) My gran enjoys pop music **even though** she is really old.
    c) My cat never wakes up **unless** he is hungry.
    d) We went for a picnic **despite** the rain.
    e) I was really tired **so** I went to bed early.
    f) My teacher told me I'd be in detention **unless** I stopped talking.
    g) The shops were all shut **as** it was a public holiday.

Q2 b) Even though she is really old, my gran enjoys pop music.
    c) Unless he is hungry, my cat never wakes up.
    d) Despite the rain, we went for a picnic.
    e) Because I was really tired, I went to bed early.
    f) Unless I stopped talking, I would be in detention.
    g) As it was a public holiday the shops were all shut.

Q3 suggested answers:
    a) David Beckham lives in Hertfordshire **even though** he plays in Manchester.
    b) The fire-eater had a day off work **as** he had a sore throat.
    c) Pollution will not decrease **until** people use their cars less.
    d) English weather is unpredictable **so** we go on holiday to Florida.
    e) He was easy to understand **until** he started speaking a language I had never heard.
    f) **As** I had broken my leg, I couldn't take part in Sports Day.

Q4 any reasonable answer

Page 55

Q1 <u>information</u>
<u>paints a picture</u>
It's hard to believe that **Bangkok is a capital city.** It's a crazy collection of <u>tranquil wats</u> (**temples**) and <u>manic markets, noisy taxis and fantastic food stalls.</u> **The most common sight though is a temple. Many people in Bangkok are Buddhists and there are temples on every street.** <u>Beautiful statues, quiet courtyards and gentle fountains can be found in every temple.</u> If you go into one of these <u>beautiful places</u>, remember to **remove your shoes as a sign of respect.**

Q2 a) iii)
    b) vi)
    c) i)
    d) v)
    e) ii)
    f) vii)
    g) iv)

Q3 any reasonable answer

Page 56

Q1 a) caption
    b) bullet points
    c) headline
    d) illustrations
    e) strapline
    f) subheading

Q2 a) underline
    b) title (larger than paragraph text)
    c) bold (for emphasis)
    d) pull-out quote — larger font, bold
    e) italic

Q3 any reasonable answer

Section 12 — Writing to Persuade

Page 57

Q1 possible answers:
    a) Animal testing is <u>pointless</u>, <u>cruel</u> and <u>heartless</u>.
    b) School uniform is <u>constricting</u>, <u>unfashionable</u> and <u>costly</u>.
    c) Action films are always <u>exciting</u>, <u>explosive</u> and <u>thrilling</u>.
    d) No one should be <u>forced</u> to wear clothes they <u>detest</u>.
    e) Animal testing is <u>vital</u> for human <u>survival</u>.
    f) Football is <u>definitely</u> the <u>most popular</u> sport in the world.
    g) We <u>all</u> get a sense of <u>pride</u> by wearing our school uniform.
    h) Animals <u>share</u> this planet with <u>us</u>.
    i) <u>Everyone</u> should make an effort to recycle.

Q2 possible answers:
    a) tedious
    b) beneficial
    c) tuneless, overrated
    d) funky, rhythmical
    e) healthy, enjoyable, invigorating
    f) embarrassing, useless, tiring
    g) rough, hard-hitting, bruising
    h) lush, peaceful, breathtaking

Q3 any reasonable answer

Q4 possible answers:
    b) None of us would wish our own pets to be experimented on.
    c) We all hate wearing uniform because we look like everyone else.
    d) School uniform is good because we are all wearing the same as everyone else.
    e) We all wish our school uniform was trendier.
    f) We all believe that the age rating on films is often wrong.
    g) We all know that we would like more facilities where we live.

Page 58

Q1 The correct order is: c), b), a), f), d), e)

Q2 The correct order is: b), d), f), a), c), e)

Q3 possible answers:
    b) Do teenagers really need to sit so many exams?
    c) Does watching videos really cause violence?
    d) Have you ever seen a film that lives up to the book?
    e) Wouldn't you prefer the comfort of designer labels?
    f) Wouldn't you rather go somewhere hot than stay in rainy Britain?
    g) Don't you think dropping litter shows no respect for our

The Answers

environment?
h) Who can afford to constantly upgrade their games console at these inflated prices?

Page 59

Q1 a) iii)   b) ii)
    c) v)   d) i)
    e) vi)   f) iv)

Q2 any reasonable answers

Q3 any reasonable answers

Page 60

Q1 any reasonable answers— for example:
   b) It is a good idea to make a cup of tea for your parents if you want extra pocket money.
   c) It would be safer to always look carefully before you cross a busy road.
   d) It would be advisable to make sure your homework is completed on time.
   e) You should try to clean your teeth at least twice a day.
   f) Try not to forget your best friend's birthday.
   g) It would be better to always wear clean socks when you are buying new shoes.
   h) To be safe it's wise to wear sunscreen to protect your skin.

Q2 any reasonable answer

Q3 possible answers:
   a) Why don't you get some advice from your subject teacher?
   b) Have you thought about taking up a team sport?
   c) Will you think about your option choices carefully?
   d) What about asking for your parents' opinions?
   e) Could you consider eating healthily?
   f) How about attending the options evening next week?
   g) Do you think you should walk to school instead of going on the bus?

Q4 any reasonable answer

Q5 any reasonable answer

Section 13 — Critical Writing

Page 61

Q1 1: therefore
       as can be seen
       furthermore
       consequently
       hence
       accordingly
       so
    2: whereas
       on the other hand
       however
       but
       conversely
       conflictingly
       in contrast
       in contradiction

Q2 list 1: a), d), e)
    list 2: b), c), f)

Q3 any reasonable answer

Q4 facts: a), c), d), h)

Page 62

Q1 any reasonable answers — for example:
   b) Boxing is a dangerous sport as many boxers suffer bad injuries.
   c) Teenagers watch far too much television.
   d) Year 9 did exceptionally well in their SATS thanks to brilliant teaching.
   e) Most teenagers get a staggering £5 a week for doing nothing.
   f) Chips taste far better than rabbit food.
   g) Amazingly, half the population still don't have a computer at home.
   h) So many young drivers means the roads are a dangerous place.

Q2 a) Mark says, "Pocket money should be £5," and I agree.
   b) In the passage it states that "working is essential to promote independence".
   c) 'The Sun' has the largest circulation, and we're told that "around 4 million copies are sold each day".
   d) Slogans for products can be easily remembered; "Just do it" for Nike is one example.
   e) The writer believes that "60% of all advertising" is aimed at children.

Q3 a) ii) b) v) c) iv) d) viii) e) iii) f) i)
    g) vi) h) vii)

Page 63

Q1 a) 'moon shone brightly'
   b) 'tree bending' / 'wind pushed' / 'branches to the ground'

Q2 facts: "the testing of cosmetics and toiletries on animals was finally banned in the UK on November 16th"
    "Of the 2.6 million experiments carried out last year, only 1319 were for testing cosmetics."
    "3 million animals"
    "animals feel pain and fear"

    opinions: "tormented in the name of science"
    "they are poisoned, scalded, wounded and killed"

Q3 any reasonable answer, e.g. "Why should they suffer?"

Q4 a) i), iv), v), vii)
    b) any reasonable answer

Section 14 — Writing About Drama

Page 64

Q1 a) mime
    b) role-play
    c) improvisation
    d) script

Q2 a) We worked in groups to produce a script.
    b) A group of us improvised a scene from a typical school day.
    c) It was very difficult to do this mime because I kept wanting to speak.
    d) After reading 'Macbeth' we put Macbeth on trial for the murder of Duncan. I role-played Lady Macbeth.
    e) Someone else wrote the script for the play, we just performed it.
    f) One of the actresses forgot her lines, so she had to improvise as she went along.

Q3 any reasonable answers. Here are some suggestions:
    a) role-play
    b) improvisation
    c) scripted performance
    d) mime
    e) role-play, improvisation, scripted performance

Page 65

Q1 e)

Q2 any reasonable answer. Here are two examples of the kind of things you could write:
    A: (nervously pacing) I was going to tell you.
    B: (stamps foot) So where is it then?

Q3 any reasonable answer

Page 66

Q1 any reasonable answers

Q2 a) set
    b) costumes
    c) lighting
    d) sound effects
    e) sound track
    f) camera angle
    g) special effects
    h) props
    i) make-up
    j) computer animation

Q3 any reasonable answer

The Answers